D0866162

Pat Patrick

African American Cultural Theory and Heritage

Series Editor: William C. Banfield

The Jazz Trope: A Theory of African American Literary and Vernacular Culture, by Alfonso W. Hawkins Jr., 2008.

In the Heart of the Beat: The Poetry of Rap, by Alexs D. Pate, 2009.

George Russell: The Story of an American Composer, by Duncan Heining, 2010.

Cultural Codes: Makings of a Black Music Philosophy, by William C. Banfield, 2010.

Willie Dixon: Preacher of the Blues, by Mitsutoshi Inaba, 2011.

Representing Black Music Culture: Then, Now, and When Again?, by William C. Banfield, 2011.

The Black Church and Hip-Hop Culture: Toward Bridging the Generational Divide, edited by Emmett G. Price III, 2012.

The Black Horn: The Story of Classical French Hornist Robert Lee Watt, by Robert Lee Watt, 2014.

Dean Dixon: Negro at Home, Maestro Abroad, by Rufus Jones Jr., 2015.

Pat Patrick: American Musician and Cultural Visionary, by Bill Banfield, 2016.

Pat Patrick

American Musician
and Cultural Visionary

Bill Banfield

ROWMAN & LITTLEFIELD
Lanham • Boulder • New York • London

Published by Rowman & Littlefield
A wholly owned subsidiary of The Rowman & Littlefield Publishing Group, Inc.
4501 Forbes Boulevard, Suite 200, Lanham, Maryland 20706
www.rowman.com

Unit A, Whitacre Mews, 26-34 Stannary Street, London SE11 4AB

British Library Cataloguing in Publication Information Available

Library of Congress Cataloging-in-Publication Data
Names: Banfield, William C., 1961–
Title: Pat Patrick : American musician and cultural visionary / Bill Banfield.
Description: Lanham : Rowman & Littlefield, 2016. | Includes bibliographical
    references and index.
Identifiers: LCCN 2016011953 (print) | LCCN 2016013194 (ebook) |
    ISBN 9781442229730 (hardcover : alk. paper) | ISBN 9781442229747 (electronic)
Subjects: LCSH: Patrick, Pat. | Jazz musicians—United States—Biography. |
    Saxophonists—United States—Biography. | LCGFT: Biographies.
Classification: LCC ML419.P44 B36 2016 (print) | LCC ML419.P44 (ebook) |
    DDC 788.7/165092—dc23
LC record available at http://lccn.loc.gov/2016011953

∞™ The paper used in this publication meets the minimum requirements of American
National Standard for Information Sciences—Permanence of Paper for Printed Library
Materials, ANSI/NISO Z39.48-1992.

Printed in the United States of America

Contents

A Note

$\mathcal{I}$ never knew my father—at least as a child would know his dad. My parents split when I was about four years old, and we had to cross a long distance of years and hard feelings before we got acquainted. I was a grown man by then, out of school, starting a career, and about to be married. My wife, Diane, whom I wanted my father to meet, was as irresistible to him as she was to me and was the conduit for our relationship until his death in 1991.

Pat Patrick the musician, the composer and arranger, the musicologist and virtuoso reed player—all that I came to know later. Of course, like anyone who ever encountered my father, I knew that music was his life. I knew that he heard music when none was evident to the ordinary ear, and that he thought about it and its origins and implications to the exclusion of almost everything else. But I didn't know or appreciate his reputation, in the Sun Ra Arkestra and beyond, until after his passing. So I am as excited about and grateful for this book as anyone.

Shortly after my father's death, my sister Rhonda, half sister La'Shon, and I traveled to his mother's home in East Moline, Illinois, to go through his effects and decide what to do with them. There were a number of his instruments, which we divided among ourselves in hopes that our children would show an interest. But mostly there were piles and piles of papers—photographs, scores, notes, and scribbles and journals.

At the time, we were too overwhelmed to deal with what we thought was the obsessive-compulsive hoarding of a life gone by. Most of it we left where it was.

Years later, not long after I was elected governor of Massachusetts, I received a call from a fellow who said he ran a storage facility in or near East Moline. He said he had several boxes of papers that seemed to contain Pat

Patrick's "stuff." He said they had been in a long-abandoned storage bin and that he had thrown them out more than once but had always gone back to retrieve the boxes and hold on to them a little longer. He could not bear to part with them. He asked if I was related to Pat Patrick and if I wanted his things.

Once the materials reached us in Massachusetts, I recalled that familiar feeling of being overwhelmed. From the abandoned storage bin in Illinois to our attic in Massachusetts? A friend suggested we offer them to Berklee College of Music. We had met Dr. William Banfield on Berklee's faculty and asked him to take a look. He did, and his expression was one of astonishment, delight, and deep appreciation.

I think it was the deep appreciation, most of all, that caused my sisters and I to donate the archives to Berklee—at least that was my motivation. Because although I didn't know my dad, clearly others did, and many others should. He was an extraordinary artist and icon of his time, and there are lessons to be learned from his story for a larger audience as well as for his son. We thank Bill for telling this tale.

—Deval Patrick, former governor of Massachusetts

Foreword

$\mathcal{W}$hen Bill Banfield and our late comrade, the genius poet Amiri Baraka, first embarked on this incredible book project, Pat Patrick would not have registered a blip on the pop culture radar. But ask any serious jazz musician or dedicated follower of this great music, and the mere mention of his name would elicit a churchlike reverence. Even before Pat Patrick's archives found their way into the able hands of Professor Banfield and his crew at Berklee College of Music, Pat Patrick's place among the great baritone saxophonists was secure, and as an alto player, he cultivated a sound all his own. He wasn't trying to be Bird or Cannonball or Dolphy. He was Pat Patrick, an American original, a musician's musician who continually reminded us that Black art is universal. Out of his horn flowed the entire history of music, from the big bands that rocked Chicago's dance halls to the R&B and blues shouters to the Afro-Latin rhythms of Mongo Santamaria to the experimental sounds of the "New Thing." Sun Ra, Thelonious Monk, Sammy Davis Jr., Earl "Fatha" Hines, Olatunji, Marvin Gaye, Patti LaBelle, 'Trane, Duke, Hawk, Cannonball. Pat Patrick was everywhere playing all kinds of music, leaving an indelible mark on our collective memory and history.

We thank Bill Banfield for this remarkable, imaginative, vivid account of Mr. Patrick's work, life, and loves.

As Patrick's longtime and devoted friend and the most important critic of Black experimental music in the twentieth century, Baraka saw Patrick's story in terms that he himself would have recognized. After all, it was Baraka who dubbed the jazz avant-garde the "new Black music," insisting that it emerged directly out of a Black tradition, bebop, as opposed to the third stream experiments of Gunther Schuller, Lee Konitz, and Lennie Tristano. Although Black musicians may have milked Western classical traditions for definitions and solutions to the "engineering" problems of contemporary jazz, Europe was not the source. "Jazz and blues," he wrote in his iconic essay "The Changing Same," "are Western musics; products of an Afro-American culture." Baraka resisted the tendency to look or listen to art for personal tragedy rather than collective memory and collective histories. And it is precisely this understanding that profoundly shaped the spirit and tone of Banfield's book—a spirit of perseverance and joy, a forward-looking vision willing to hold on to elements of the past while never succumbing to nostalgia.

Banfield, a dazzling guitarist blessed with godlike fingers, a marvelous composer, and a prolific scholar and writer in his own right, is cut from the same cloth as Patrick and Baraka. Indeed, he is a "son" of Baraka, if you will, because his music, writing, and intellect embody the principles of the "changing same." He ignores boundaries of genre and style, embracing the totality of Black music and culture in everything he does. Their collaboration, along with the Patrick's commitment to preservation and documentation, turned what might have been just another jazz biography into a genuine event, a carnival of sound and fury, tragedy and comedy, discipline, deviance and defiance, revolutionary love, and human longing.

I hope that all readers come away from *Pat Patrick: American Musician and Cultural Visionary* not only acknowledging Patrick's extraordinary contributions to modern music but recognizing the price he paid to make our lives richer and more beautiful. No one can give that much art, that much originality and creativity, for free—especially in a society where everything is a commodity, and Black life, thought, and invention is continually devalued. Patrick understood this, wrote about it, and resisted it mind, body, and soul. And in the end, he triumphed. Evidence is in his recordings, his compositions, his archive, and the very book you hold in your hands. As you now must know, each page illustrating Pat Patrick's life and work profoundly expresses the essential message of *The Cry of Jazz*, the film where he makes his visual debut of Sun Ra's Arkestra. The film not only presents Patrick quite literally blowing the blues away but speaks his essential truth, revealing what it means to triumph. As the narrator put it, "Denied a future, the joyous celebration of the present is the Negro's answer to America's ceaseless attempts to obliterate him. Jazz is the musical expression of the Negro's eternal recreation of the present."

—Robin D. G. Kelley, Gary B. Nash Professor of American
History at UCLA, author of *Thelonious Monk: The Life
and Times of an American Original* (2009)

Preface

Our job here should be to try to help in rebuilding a people's culture that yet is . . . a major source of ideas and inspiration . . . of real value . . . to the world.

—Pat Patrick, from "Yesterdays, Todays and Tomorrows," 1973

This is a story about being a musician in America, a musician who, growing up in Chicago in the 1940s, begins professionally in the 1950s, continues as a strong musical icon through the 1980s, and achieves a phenomenal number of musical accomplishments: living and recording in New York, touring internationally, gigging locally, producing musical theater, leading concerts, teaching, creating radio programs, and more. Pat Patrick is a model of the hardworking, everyday musician with aspirations and family challenges. At the end of his long race, he faces his death like a human-spirited champion. Pat Patrick is a great American musician's story. And this is the story we tell.

Pat Patrick was a saxophonist, multi–wind player, arranger, composer, music director, theater works producer, educator, and visionary. He was a musician who performed with Duke Ellington, Quincy Jones, Thelonious Monk, Mongo SantaMaria, Nat King Cole, James Moody, Eric Dolphy, Marvin Gaye, Patti LaBelle, and Billy Taylor. And for more than thirty-five years, he laid down the bottom on the baritone saxophone with the indefinable Sun Ra Arkestra. Pat Patrick is an example par excellence of American musicianship and artistry.

Any one of these identities might be enough to illuminate the meaning of musicianship. But this is also a story about American society and the meaning and costs of artistry. It's about the definition of cultural heritages. It is also about fatherhood and family and about finding and defining accomplishments. And this is a story about music.

Placing this story of Pat Patrick's artistry within the framework of Black music culture—and the larger context of human expression—requires a deeper sharing. The important lens through which this story is told belongs largely to Pat Patrick himself—his own carefully prepared archives, his personal papers, artifacts, scrapbooks, music, and news clippings, along with his more than two thousand personal photographs. Together, these illuminate one very rich view of American musicianship.

Here, biography in the traditional academic sense is redefined. This is an artistic mapping. The narrative underlining what we discovered reveals the essential components, themes, concerns, and important creative periods that thread together the story of Pat Patrick's life.

Our layout follows a narrative of activities, interspersed with incredible rich pieces from the archives—Patrick quotations, news clippings, poster performance announcements, reviews, photographs, and more. Our reflections and findings enable us to explore the productive life of this incredible musician.

Documenting and sharing the history of American creative works is critical today. Why? Because our education in the humanities is dependent upon strong examples providing foundations for human excellence. When you raise these examples up, all else follows. History, heritages, and heroes become necessary foci for the best of all we want to be and become.

Pat Patrick works within a fantastic history, a framework of twentieth-century jazz and popular music in the United States. His work comes at one of the most critical points in our social and cultural history to date—the 1960s and 1970s—when so much was rebooted, new directions were set in place, and trusted foundations set aflame. Music, musicians, and the history they reside in are some of the most poignant and powerful collections of voices that determine our paths. We are dedicated to such presentations of our history, and Pat Patrick was a champion of the great music practice that ensures our survival forward.

Acknowledgments

$\mathscr{I}$ thank the following people for their work, help, and encouragement of this book. First of all, Amiri and Amini Baraka. To Amiri for your inspiring work, then excitement and charge for carrying this book forward. This book is for you and dedicated to you. I am sorry that you are not here to see its publication. You are deeply, deeply missed.

To Governor Deval Patrick, Rhonda Patrick-Sigh, La'Shon Anthony, and the entire Patrick family, thank you for your gift of your father's archive to Berklee College of Music, with the charge that these items must be used for "educating musicians about the importance, furtherance and preservation of Black music culture."

To Rhonda and La'Shon, the view of your dad given through your rich and touching stories is immeasurable. Thank you.

To the governor, you kept me, "on beat in line, the whole time." I remain grateful. The numerous visits to your offices and the generosity and time given both to Amiri and me provided us the starting points we so greatly needed.

To Pat's sister, Sheila Miles, what a gracious and informative talk-time with you. Thank you.

To my editor, Dr. Camille Colatosti, for her continuous eye on my writings, thank you.

Again, thank you to Camille Colatosti and Phillip Kwik for their work in sorting and cataloging this incredible collection.

Many thanks to my wife, Dr. Krystal Banfield, who brought the archives to Berklee at the invitation of the governor.

Thank you to Dr. Darla Hanley, dean of the Professional Education Division of Berklee College of Music, for allowing us to store the archive in the Center for Africana Studies.

Special thanks also to Sofia Becerra-Licha, archivist at the Stan Getz Library, Berklee College of Music, for her invaluable assistance in organizing the crucial images for this book.

A very, very special thanks to Tad Hershorn and our friends at Rutgers University, Center for Jazz Studies, who provided invaluable research assistance, support, and so much of the information on Pat's workings.

To my dear friend, historian Dr. Robin Kelley, thank you for your many years of friendship, your incredible example, and commitment to deep scholarship and for turning me onto the straight paths of the Patrick interviews. Thank you, also, for your helpful insights, visits to Berklee's Center for Africana Studies, and for teaching us all.

To the Rowman & Littlefield family, thank you for your tireless devotion and encouragement of my books, the African American Cultural Heritage Series, and your creative commitment to meaningful scholarship that reaches out to all.

Portrait of Pat Patrick
From the Pat Patrick Archive

Interviews with Pat Patrick's Son and Daughters

> It took the so-called revolutionary atmosphere just for me to be able to play for my folks again. That to me is progress.
>
> —From the Pat Patrick Archives

*W*e began our interviews with son Deval Patrick and daughters Rhonda Sigh and La'Shon Anthony, asking them, "How do want your father's work to be seen and appreciated?" We thought it was important to begin the biography this way in order to try and get a sense for how the family felt their father's work should best be presented. From those frank discussions, we were able to draw important themes and begin to trace Pat Patrick's musical workings from his early days with Sun Ra, flowering for thirty years into his very busy performance schedule in which he led his own numerous ensembles, as well as recorded and performed with, among others, Duke Ellington, Cab Calloway, Earl Fatha Hines, Clarke Terry, Quincy Jones and His Orchestra, Thelonious Monk, Mongo SantaMaria, Nat King Cole, James Moody, Pearl Bailey, Cannonball Adderley, Eric Dolphy, Marvin Gaye, Patti LaBelle, and Billy Taylor. We learned that Patrick also arranged scores and worked on off-Broadway shows; he led radio programs; he wrote and edited essays; he traveled and he taught. The interviews with the family confirmed that Pat Patrick was a quintessential example of American productive artistry. His paths were wide.

Bill Banfield and Amiri Baraka: Tell us about your father.

Rhonda Sigh: Well, we know that music was Dad's first love. And he served that community well. Not only through physical talent, he tried to bring Black culture together through his philosophy, his wisdom, and understanding of how the Black community could be better through music. He wanted to "better" the culture.

I think focusing on the music would be a great way to honor him. I don't mean to disregard what he was as a father but make it about his music and how he contributed to it. Music was definitely first for him.

I loved him and appreciated him for this. We never held any grudges against him. As a matter of fact, he would apologize, constantly for not being there. Especially as we got older, he recognized he made a mistake.

Deval Patrick: A story about Dad's music and the contributions he made to music is really important. To him, there was the technical fluency, but it was music in a group context, about how it moved the group, historically and culturally, where it could take us. I do think music is a passion for him. It is about the science of music, the artistry of it, but also music as a social tool.

Rhonda Sigh: The story should also be about how your experiences in life prompt the kind of music you put out. How his separation from his kids, feeling bad about that, brings out a kind of expression, a tune. I'm sure this is true with all musicians—life affects the art.

Deval Patrick: I agree. Even though they were apart, he wrote a song for Rhonda called "Miss Loophy."

Rhonda Sigh: He was the wisest man I've ever known. I never considered that he was so political or had these thoughts on politics and policies. But he would give little hints [that] these were things that were on his mind.

Amiri Baraka: What was your take on that whole period? What was your conception of Black power?

Rhonda Sigh: I had a strong sense of his Black American cultural interests.

Deval Patrick: As I looked at the material in his folders, I realized he was a pack rat. It's a wonder! He was constantly making records because he knew he had something to say. I think he saw himself as a student, observer, and commentator of the times and a voice that was not appreciated at the time. I think he was organizing his own thoughts and writing for a larger audience. He would keep notes of the scolding he would give us as kids. I think he understood the centrality of Black culture. The way Black people speak to each other; Africans-speak. And some of those messages from him at the time, I appreciated.

Amiri Baraka: Do you think he was able to pass on to you any musical aspirations?

Rhonda Sigh: There was a feeling that he was a special musician. But we didn't feel it until we were adults. The impact that he made on me was how he made me appreciative of the music all around. I was an aspiring dancer, and they put me onstage.

Deval Patrick: I didn't think of him as a cultural figure. And I struggled with that because of us not knowing him. I didn't appreciate how important of a musician he was until I was in college.

I remember one time, when I was in law school, a friend of mine said, "I've got every album he's been on." Pat's influence made me think differently about what musicians are doing. I had no idea about Sun Ra. I began to understand at that point, but it wasn't accessible to me. Sun Ra is an acquired taste. You really have to understand the music to understand Sun Ra.

Pat Patrick's Parents
From the Pat Patrick Archive

My father was born in East Moline, in western Illinois. His mother was Lavern Love, and his father was Laurdine Patrick Sr. He was himself a professional trumpeter. His parents lived on a farm in Colorado. My grandparents met on the railroads, in the Quad Cities, the adjacent and across-the-river cities of Rock Island, East Moline, and Moline, Illinois, plus Davenport, Iowa. They then moved to Chicago.

Pat went to Dusable High School, on Chicago's south side, with Captain Walter Dyett, his band director. My father would talk about Walter Dyett.

In maybe a dozen conversations I've had with my father, Dyett was one of the related things he would come back to. He talked about his insistence that musicians master their art, the rules, the customs, the classics. That they practice. My father's extraordinary discipline around his music came from Captain Dyett.

My father's understanding of classical music theory was as rich as Yo-Yo Ma! Because that was what was expected. He understood symphonic music, music structure, and theory. And the practicing was on that.

He knew you had to master this in order to break out on "the new frontier." By the time he graduated from high school, he wanted to become a professional musician.

My father met my mother in high school. She dropped out, and they had my sister in 1955. He came to know Sun Ra during this time, and by 1960, they split and he moved to New York. Of all the people he played with, it was [Thelonious] Monk who sticks out. He loved Monk, but he used to say that Monk wouldn't rehearse.

Near his death, he moved back to East Moline to be closer to home. He wanted his ashes spread in the Mississippi.

Knowing how much stuff we have not recovered for the archives—wow. When I was doing trial work, I would write down the chronology and the source material for things day by day, the events. Sometimes those juxtapositions tell you things. One impression I have had of Pat is he had tensions between the artistry of music and the commercial part of it. The resentment had to do with feeling he was being taken advantage of, how it impinged upon the art. His view of art was almost "romantic." I mean the right way to be a true artist and not to have commercialism tarnish that.

This comes hit-and-miss from him. But this seems to be an issue of integrity for him. This is not a new story of trying to figure out how to live. But this seems to be something that bothered him. He didn't feel he was getting his due commercial reward.

Amiri Baraka: The normal antagonism is one thing, but when you are Black, he's carrying that around, too, as a double measure.

Deval Patrick: He would listen to some musical phrase in the Beatles, for instance, and he knew it from his study. It had roots that he had connections to.

Amiri Baraka: When Pat comes to New York, it is just when these things are "coming up in smoke." So this is the added whip to it. Then he turned to Sun Ra, because Sun Ra is a portrait of that integrity of art, purity of spirit as an artist. But this is the core of a long conversation for Pat: what are the forces that he is reacting to as an artist of integrity and as a Black person. I know this bothered him; it bothered all of us. Pat wanted to make this struggle identifiable to people.

Bill Banfield: Pat has to decide what compromises to make in order to eat. But he is transcribing the music of the day. So he's conversant with the language of the day as well.

Deval Patrick: If the book doesn't do anything else, it must decode this classic tension with race in America in the 1960s and 1970s. It's deep and sizzling.

Amiri Baraka: When you got together then with a group of musicians, this is what they were talking about.

Bill Banfield: Can you explain? What is the "this" that Pat has urgency about?

Deval Patrick: It was this phrase, "the capitalism part," that is the *this* that fuels the urgency in part because it intrudes on his art, and it [also] doesn't reward his art.

Amiri Baraka: To be poor and dismissed and then feeling that you are some kind of a vex on society is a hot subject. One thing also you can see is Pat's "national consciousness," as well as his rebellious stance toward all "ready-mades," even religion and various traditionalisms. He had no patience for those who did not question and innovate.

Daughter La'Shon Anthony visited the Pat Patrick archives in April 2013. She brought her two sons, eighteen and twenty years old at the time, to inspect their grandfather's collection and to issue the final family challenge.

La'Shon Anthony: The family appreciates the maintenance of Pat's archives by Berklee and this published biography. The reality is Pat had a double life. He had great musical talents, expertise, and learned to command numerous instruments. But he was an extremely disconnected person with his family, which I find odd. As I hear artists talk, the majority of them say they go to countries to be among the people, their dances, music, and culture. He had very close bonds with musicians, but was estranged from his family. Most people put family first. I don't know what happened to him to change his interactions, making him find comfort and support with outside parties.

Obviously something happened. But as a child, this was not a question for me to ask. As I became older, it did not matter. He and I had a civil relationship. I do find it surprising, though, that now twenty years after his death, his body of work is still so important over other deserving peers during his time.

Bill Banfield: These questions about why Pat's work is so important, why now, and what made Pat Patrick a subject of interest in music are the questions many others will have as well. These are the questions that continue to move this inquiry. We started this book as a family story, and we wanted to tell it that way. We explored these story points, these facts of Pat Patrick's life crossroads, and how these intersected with his music.

Biographies are launched among many moving parts within and on the subject's life. But we felt these questions were important to help to make Pat's story meaningful to everyday readers as well. But let's be clear, Pat Patrick was no ordinary sideman musician. He was not an afterthought or secondary. He was an extraordinary musician by all accounts whose artistic and musical prowess, as well as his intellectualism and conceptualism, stand high among the greatest of musicians of his era. Pat Patrick was one of those great historical figures who deserves a chapter in *the* American music history book.

The archival materials are stunning in detail and scope and, in a way, they are the star component of this book. They were originally collected, assembled, and stored personally by Pat Patrick. With that charge and accountability, we attempted to frame Pat Patrick's life in relation to the mainframe of jazz activity, viewing his position as a critical player among important musical figures in American history.

· 2 ·

Introduction to Pat Patrick
An American Musician

Music is a high medium of art. There can be no disputing the rapid communicative properties of music and its ability to reach all people. Therefore, high standards should be maintained by its practitioners and high values by its adherents if music is to weave its magic spell.

—Pat Patrick, from *Yesterdays, Todays and Tomorrows*, 1973

Of all the musicians who have inspired me over the years, Pat Patrick represents one of the most full bodied and impressive. I was honored to get the opportunity to explore his rich musical life. Doubling that honor was the opportunity to discover his life more deeply by working on this biography with the great Amiri Baraka. Mr. Baraka was also one of Pat Patrick's best friends.

A friend and scholar, Genna Rae McNeal, admonished me to be sure that I think about "the framing and approach [of this biography] very carefully." The real-life story of how a person lived and what they lived for is important stuff. It matters. I began then reading biographies more closely and appreciating that sometimes nuanced story, that real life, and what matters both to the subject and to the world around the subject, the artist. I was sure that the lessons from my writing partner, Amiri Baraka, would be exacting and exhilarating. His guiding hand and ideas would be a tradition's weight of worth.

Amiri Baraka, as a leading literary arts figure, historian, and aesthetician, would be like a life raft as I could see myself struggling through the waves of this literary and cultural assignment. Writing a biography is a special kind of narrative journey. A special ear, eye, nose, dance, and overview on the subjects of human personality, persistence, preservation, and purpose are embodied in the task of telling someone's life story in the arts.

7

I prefer to think of this as a creative life narrative focused on the exploration of a working musician and the implications of that expressive life in connection with other musicians, the real world, and the cultural context that supports—or does not support—the expressive life. I was reading other biographies and saw that Robin Kelley, in his *Thelonious Monk*, framed each chapter with quotations that spiraled outward to illuminate the life of the artist. Approached as revolving within a community of family, musician friends, and Kelley's own appreciation of the Monk figure, the work is a masterful telling from a passionate perspective. Both biographies on Samuel Coleridge Taylor and Scott Joplin, by authors Geoffrey Self and Edward Berlin, were written to lay out simply the specific creative chapters chronologically of the artists' lives. Terry Teachout's work on Pops Satchmo outlines the cultural context, highlighting the world the new king had to walk in and how he remolded that world and created a new musical language to speak in it. Leonard Bernstein's biography, as told by author Humphrey Burton, reads, "and so ended the last chapter in the life of one of the most remarkable and flamboyant artists and towering musical presences of the twentieth century. . . . He truly belonged to the world." This helps to frame Bernstein's larger-than-life, artistic personal demeanor, as well as the personality, the dynamic enigma that underlines the book's focus and principle interest.

Passionate perspective, family, artistry, chronological artistic development, cultural contexts, and themes consistently marked my consciousness as I tried to heed my colleague's earlier warning that a biography must be carefully crafted to frame the real-life study of Pat Patrick, American musician.

Thus, this creative life narrative recounts how Pat Patrick lived as a musician and what he lived for, what he believed, what music he made, and for whom he made it. These are our guiding themes.

Additionally, we have at our disposal the Pat Patrick Archive, a gift from the Patrick family to Berklee College of Music for the purpose of the study of Black music and in honor of the life of their father. This collection consists of personal materials, music scores, more than two thousand photographs, recordings, personal papers, family correspondences, Pat Patrick's will, music and theatric productions, newspaper clippings, and reviews. These materials provide an extraordinary view of the life and work of this dedicated, focused, and impassioned musician, and they provide much of the content that guides this book.

Through the archive, which acts as a window to the wide artistic world of Pat Patrick, we sought to craft a narrative that brings focus and attention to this important musician, whose story had not yet been told. This is important, we think, not only because Patrick's story should be told, but also because his narrative reveals the fuller story of American musicianship and artistry. This is a story seen by following the lives of everyday working musicians, people like Patrick. Every bandleader is given sound only through the work of his or her supportive musicians. In the case of Patrick, he was, for thirty-plus years, a sideman, a supporting musician, arranger, and concert promoter of many well-known musicians.

There is Pat Patrick the musician, the thinker, the teacher/educator, the businessperson, the arranger, and the archivist. There is as well Pat Patrick the flawed father, a musician who fathered children and yet chose to live closer to music than to his family but was haunted by his absence from his children. In a song written in 1969 for his eldest daughter and firstborn (b. 1955), "Miss Loophy," which refers to her nickname, the lyrics state,

> Loophy, why do you haunt me so, where I go. I waste time dreaming night and day of you, and wondering how to forget you. Still hearing the song in your voice, I see that smile and know all the while, it's Loophy, the child-like way you glow. You mean so much to me, you know.

And although these words were arranged to pass for a torch ballad, it has "I love my little girl" all over it in both text and sentiment. It is a gorgeous ballad both in harmonic content and melodic construction and flow. It sings.

This was an interesting detail to find, because music sings the deep meanings that matter. Through this song, we see Pat Patrick's regret for his estrangement from his children. And so the music, the mission, and what matters, too, becomes all the more a musical score with many cadences, key changes, and a part of the compelling story.

This is the story of Pat Patrick, one fabulous working musician who played with famous people and in that supporting team-player role, became a great model for what is meant by being a great American musician.

Pat Patrick: American Musician and Cultural Visionary is a biography grounded in the view of the world seen through a musician's eyes, a world shaped by Black music and characterized by Patrick's progressive critique of American society during a challenging period in U.S. history. Music and society here are partners in a play shaping our unique social creative history. Pat Patrick is a participant in that evolution, and this is his story.

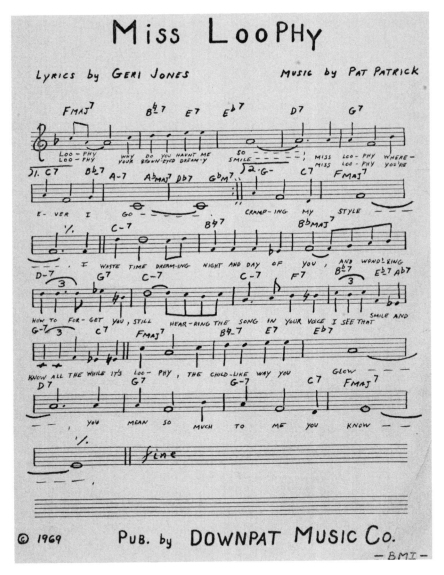

"Miss Loophy" Sheet Music
From the Pat Patrick Archive

• _3_ •

Life and Ideas

And Mr. Patrick had the most old-fashioned tone-reedy sound
with a wide vibrato—and the most modern ear. In a solo on his
own Duke Ellington–flavored ballad, "Little Nieces," he implied
advanced harmonies in confident, asymmetrical phrases.

—*New York Times*, August 1983

_P_at Patrick is an example par excellence of American musicianship and artistry. He was a saxophonist, multi-wind player, arranger, composer, music director, theater works producer, teacher, and visionary. Any one of these titles
or identities might be enough to illuminate the meaning of great American
musicianship. But his artistry came from within grand Black music culture
and stretched outward to embrace and define the larger context of American
life. Patrick's legacy reveals interconnections among life, music, and culture.
This is a legacy that is, on one hand, timeless and, on the other, very much
connected to the time in which Patrick lived.

As Patrick himself wrote, "What America, particularly the younger set,
is just beginning to understand and appreciate, what the rest of the world has
been aware of to a greater degree, is the universality of Black Afro-American
music." This idea and others are the focus of this biography. We look at
Patrick's interpretation of his creative work with special emphasis on his
most prolific period, approximately between 1960 and 1985. His materials,
letters, writings, and photographs are the real stars of this sharing, as they,
beyond the narrative, provide a rich window into the life and work of this
great American artist.

Let's continue with his 1973 essay, "Our Music, Yesterdays, Todays
and Tomorrows." Here, Pat Patrick took on the persona of a narrator named
Akbadiwn, who reveals,

11

Herein are a few thoughts about our Musical Art Form, which I have been involved with most of my so-called life, that I hope will clear away some of the fog of misconception surrounding the same. . . . Having walked it, talked it, ate it, slept it, wept it and kept it, for the better part of thirty years, mostly as a scuffling, Black musician on a so-called professional level in this economic-orientated society, I can testify to how messed up the music scene is, if nothing else. How I relate what I have seen and experienced will be for real, if not always understood. Fortunately, those things I learned by trial and error have afforded me a better insight with less frustration about what I see happening in the world with regard to Black music.

As mentioned, Patrick's most productive professional years came when he was in his thirties and forties, during the musically expressive, albeit turbulent, years of the 1960s and 1970s. For him, as for many musicians in that era, heeding a "call" to their time was as important as the music that was being called up. Patrick writes in this same essay, "Our job here should be to try to help in rebuilding a people's culture that has been prostrated, adulterated, and raped for centuries and yet is, in this so-called space age, still a major source of ideas and inspiration. Proving to all of reasonable mentality that it is of real value, not just to the people through whom it has come, but to the world."

The three themes that surface—"our job, responsibility"; "rebuilding the people's culture"; and uplifting the music as "a major source of ideas and inspiration"—underline Patrick's commitment as a Black musician to the music of yesterday, today, and tomorrow. His story is focused through the lens of what it means to be a musician in his time, creating music that holds the musician accountable to the people and that has the potential to carry ideas and inspiration.

As we begin to dig deeper, we find that it's a wide, rich, and sustainable story with many floors. This story is about Pat Patrick. But as well, it's a story about American society and the meaning and costs of artistry. It is a story about the definition and furtherance of cultural heritages, and it is a story about great musicianship. It is also about fatherhood and family and finding and defining accomplishment. And it's a story about music.

Patrick's story is, of course, a personal one, the story of an individual who sought to make a difference and to create a life of music and artistry that connected to his time. But the story is also a social one. Situating Pat Patrick, his work, and his beliefs about music and culture in the vitally interesting period in which he lived helps us better understand his life and our own lives. We can see that his ideas, successes, and struggles had great consequence for how we see ourselves today. Pat Patrick is a father who knows family, and he joins a "father-like figure"—Sun Ra—who builds a musician's family and community. As a father seeking to be a musician, as someone who struggles with relationships in his own family, he reveals a complex and yet compelling dynamic. As well, his forty-year close association with Sun Ra is essential to understanding his life and his place in his musician family. His relationship with Sun Ra is substantive and was sustained from 1949 through the 1980s and beyond. This alone is a most remarkable association in terms of professional artistry, personal dynamics, and meaning.

At the same time, if we are not careful on this journey, we can be swept into the Sun Ra orbit. Sun Ra's work and cult following among fans, music pundits, and aficionados is legendary. Sun Ra is an orbiting entity—huge—but in a way, self-orbiting. So immediately you have to ask, how did this well-rounded, grounded, deeply prepared musician, Pat Patrick, recruited by Sun Ra, find the ability to break free and establish his own identity and path?

We became interested in the Patrick "breakout" from the Sun Ra orbit. This became one of the compelling questions when separating out the various parts of the voluminous musician work patterns of Pat Patrick's life. Given these pieces, we have a compelling story to tell.

DREAMS AND MISSIONS THAT MATTERED

When we read biographies, we find ourselves wondering about the circumstances that help to define a life story. As we began this journey, we looked for breaking moments, moments of tragedy and triumph that revealed key themes. In the case of Pat Patrick, there is the sense that he was a great musician defined by a series of forces beyond himself. Why? Because his musical career starts from the same soil as Louis Armstrong, Muddy Waters, Nat King Cole, Chuck Berry, Quincy Jones, and Sun Ra, all of whom were musicians who lived during a period in Chicago or had moved there from the South to become a part of music's future, shaping it as they went along. Patrick had all of these forces upon him and was part of a great musical movement in Chicago. As he wrote, "Chicago at that time was on the ebb of one of the greatest musical episodes in the history of African American music that there has probably ever been."

He moved, like millions of others, to this cultural mecca exploding at the time for Black people. It was the Chicago of the 1940s and 1950s. He went to a high school where famous musicians had attended. He lived in a city that again had famous musicians and fabulous places to play music. Then he landed in a band with a man who claimed to be writing the future.

He steps as an adult into a decade, the 1960s, that was to determine in many ways the future. In a way, he and his bandmates became the future.

And so, as a talented musician with a dream and a mission playing under a leader who was mission control during a time when musicians' dreams and missions mattered, for Pat Patrick, things mattered.

He wrote,

> We should begin to pay more attention to our common sayings and street sayings and from where and how it comes into being. Such as, "Black poems," "Right on," and the much-popularized hand slap that's been a tradition among Black men for a long time, and what we see on the football, basketball, and other sports fields. These days, they, like other things of our heritage, are constantly being used and exploited by no less "the big commercial enterprises" to push and sell their products on TV, radio, etc. And why? Because "our thing" gives "their thing" that human quality that makes them attractive to the prospective buyer.

MUSIC AND IDEAS: SOME OF THE MOST IMPORTANT MUSIC WE HAVE EVER HEARD

We spent months mentally preparing to work on the life of Pat Patrick as a biography. But, as mentioned, it is impossible to consider Pat Patrick's life without walking through the life and music of Sun Ra. And so we began to listen to this music more deeply. We certainly were familiar with the 1972 *Space Is the Place* album, and we knew the film performances from the 1970s. Then we saw *The Cry of Jazz*, the 1956 film for which Sun Ra provided the "soundtrack." We heard something that we had not heard before, a 1956 example of a well-tuned bebop-ish big band, not much different from Billy Eckstein, or Duke, even. And there was Pat Patrick prominently featured. This was the first time we saw him in a film with the band before 1960. This film was the living world out of which came the 1956 to 1969 recordings on Sun Ra's label, Saturn. This music is some of the most important music to be heard from this period for many reasons.

These recordings and performances—*Angels and Demons* (1956), *The Nubians of Plutinia* (1958–1959), *Fate in a Pleasant Mood* (1960), *When the Sun Comes Out* (1961), *When Angels Speak of Love* (1963), *The Magic City* (1965), *Atlantis* (1967–1969)—are already in the language of where jazz was heading, as it was redefining itself as "more modern," post-bebop. Immediately, the music sounds distinctive in concept, approach, and sonorities. Sun Ra's piano approach, voicings, and his styling are evident. The originality of the music from this period is striking, as is the diversity of traditions; this new jazz includes ballads, blues, bebop swinging blues, and "free jazz," all mixed comfortably.

But the "voice of the Arkestra" is there, and it is clear that this is music that is consciously defining another direction. Any time that happens, it is important. *Angels and Demons* comes before Mingus, before Ellington's experimental suites, before the Art Ensemble of Chicago, before Gunther's Third Stream, before Gil Evans's later works, before George Russell, before Frank Zappa, before Cecil Taylor. When you hear these works, orchestrations with bells, gongs, global instruments, oboes and bass clarinets in the lines, synthesizers, timpani drums, and the line conception, you know this is music from another place and that it is going in another direction. It strikes you as different yet familiar.

That's noteworthy. In Sun Ra, you hear Ellington, Monk, and Mingus all in one and yet something very different. These are some of the most beautiful, freshly adventuresome ensemble works we have ever heard. The piece "Travel the Spaceways from Planet to Planet," a funky monotone, almost free jazz–sounding work, prophetically prepares all for what was to happen, a decade before Apollo 11.

"Calling Planet Earth" is actually a concerto for Pat Patrick, akin to Ellington's Concerto for Cootie. Pat Patrick became a staple and exemplified what New York critics called Sun Ra's "energy music" performance. This work from these 1956 through 1961 performances is a model piece that links Pat Patrick essentially to his first pathbreaking act in the revolutionary Sun Ra band as a performing and recording artist. Patrick's voice, contribution, and potential forward are most evident, providing us with a musical pathway. The Sun Ra Arkestra, by the 1970s, when all his stars were in full orbit, had already been a practicing ensemble since the late 1940s. So, to a large extent, the band of the 1950s in Chicago fits first into the traditional big band jazz door.

Sun Ra arrived on the New York scene in the 1960s with a well-oiled recording and cosmology machine, at the same time when the world was exploring space travel, as in the Apollo 11 moon landing in 1969. By the late 1970s entered the movies *Star Wars* (1977) and *Close Encounters of the Third Kind* (1977), helping to make Sun Ra's image well-suited for the 1970s imagination and quests for intergalactic encounters. Sun Ra was even asked by *Esquire* in July 1969—along with Muhammad Ali and a list of who's who including Hubert Humphrey, Senator George McGovern, Ed Koch, Bob Hope, W. H. Auden, and Gwendolyn Brooks—what he thought of the space voyage, and he blessed them with a sun poem:

> Reality has touched against myth
> Humanity can move to achieve the impossible
> Because when you've achieved one impossible the others come together
> To be with their brother, the first impossible.
> . . . Happy Space Age to you[1]

Sun Ra's band now foreshadows Earth Wind and Fire's *Egyptology* and the costumes of Parliament Funkadelic and Sly Stone.

Sun Ra's band members also participated in the aesthetic door of another movement, orbiting simultaneously in the cultural musical landscape of the 1960s and 1970s—the jazz avant-garde, what Amiri Baraka and others called "the new thing." Like Ornette Coleman, Albert Ayler, Archie Schepp, and John Coltrane, who also joined a label, in this case, Impulse Records, known to the world as the company that carried new jazz forward, Sun Ra Arkestra could be counted firmly in the now of contemporary jazz circles.

Sun Ra was also a part of the Black nationalist movements that included the Black Muslims, the Black Panthers, and the Black Arts movement. And although Sun Ra should not be confused as advocating Black nationalist ideologies, as many mistakenly thought, his respect for Egypt and ancient Africa and his spirituality made him appear to be advocating a civil rights agenda. But his agenda was always the future, or outer space. The mysteries of Sun Ra! He said in the film *Space Is the Place* (1974), "The people have no music that is in coordination with their spirits . . . because of this, they are out of tune with the universe." In another earlier interview, he stated,

> Music is an example. . . . If you are the musician which you should be, and you intervene where it is necessary, and you were to play with a maximum of precision and discipline . . . you can lean on something that is firm and the music will come out good enough. . . . The people could sound magnificent if they had the correct composer or arranger who would know how to judiciously use them to make them play together and obtain a certain sound.[2]

His "outer space dimension/cosmological musicology" entered all of the band members, and for Pat Patrick, who in fact has a Black nationalist sentiment, it takes another form, as Patrick described in his notes "the universality of the Black Afro-American music." This is one indication among Patrick's writings that this allegiance to a sociocultural earthly concern for Blackness is nonetheless derivative from Sun Ra. We are reminded of a statement by a local pastor who said, "What you gonna do with that gift that calls on your life?"

All the people we watch in greatness look at music as a through-line, art-life existence, a ritual, a history, a cultural voice, their faith or ministry toward people, a deeply engaged endeavor, and a life commitment and pursuit. They die for their music and die in it. The statement, "the people have no music that is in coordination with their spirits . . . because of this they are out of tune with the universe," was so real for Sun Ra, Coltrane, Patrick, and others from this period.

Patrick saw music as a high-order discipline, able to take the chaos out of the world and retune people into their humanity. As he wrote in his "Article to Honor Educators,"

> In music as in everything else a person desires to do and do well, basic training is very important. Of course the type of basic training can differ and the types of practitioners produced will vary. But if in the main, they strive towards the artistic expression this in itself will speak of the type of basic training that was adhered to. Then too this gets to be another issue and problem when the masses get to the point where they can't distinguish between art and junk. Too often we are exposed to more junk than art and consequently our tastes begin to adhere to more junk. This comes from a lack of exposure to the real thing. Then you can see where those who have never been exposed to real music will be coming from. This is called false or "jive indoctrination."

The major themes of Pat Patrick as a thinker, from his essays, notes, and letters, orbit in and around this kind of "special-ness in the music," and focus on these topics:

- Black musical art form
- the "messed-up" music scene
- conspiracy
- heritage
- value
- music as a medium of high art
- high standards
- musicians as "light bearers"
- the need for Black people to know, understand, and appreciate their heritage
- real music, which he defines as inspiring, spontaneous, and stimulating versus "jive music," or fake commercial music

All of these ideas can be found as themes in Sun Ra's philosophy, as well, and it is here that we see the influence of Sun Ra on Pat Patrick's aesthetic and cultural development. Sun Ra is curiously discussed as "relevant" by some European avant-garde thinkers like German composer Karl Stockhausen, for instance. And Sun Ra's band and music hits the center of at least five or six aesthetic circles of musical- and cultural-consciousness values at a time when music and culture was expanding its own territories through experimentation with sociopolitical ideas and movements. Few other musicians' music coexisted in that kind of ripe musical context. So Pat Patrick and the band members were participants in a unique phenomenon.

Pat Patrick was member number two of the original Sun Ra Chicago ensemble, a contributing and central mechanism. He was a core voice to the music of Sun Ra, and this work ultimately shaped his ideas as a musician, as it did for Sun Ra. As John Szwed wrote of Sun Ra's workings,

> He might also be remembered as a composer in the great tradition, one who was driven by a hunger for totality that only music could express. To him poetry, dance, and music were linked together as arts of the immediate means for engaging the emotions with a higher reality. . . . He understood music to be more than feelings about phenomena; it could express its essence, and reveal the true nature of the world. Sun Ra saw that music symbolized the unity in diversity that is the cosmos, and the big band was his space vehicle, African American aesthetics his culture synthesizing principle. He was a band leader as prophetic leader, the music arranger as arranger of the world.[3]

Pat Patrick was definitely immersed and inspired by these concepts. Sun Ra was his musical father, the final mentor from whom Patrick would emerge as a working musician, arranger, band leader and teacher throughout the late 1950s through the 1960s, 1970s, and 1980s, until his passing. After being chosen as the second member of the Sun Ra band, Pat Patrick became in New York a polished musician who would exemplify these practices as normative.

· *4* ·

Developing as a Musician, 1949–1960

The system today is basically the same system that was instituted when this country was founded. Slavery was a part of that system's makeup because it was found to be profitable. That same system functions the same way and people are involved in it, knowingly or not, because of its monetary profits and economic gains. It is as much American as apple pie or hotdogs. And the masses of people exist according to their positions in it.

—Pat Patrick, from notes

THE BEGINNINGS

If we follow this story mostly as an overview, a line of playing from the point at which Pat graduated from Chicago's Dusable High in 1949—remember that he is from the Quad Cities region, also home to Bix Biderbecke and Louie Bellson—we see Pat Patrick on a solid, forty-year track as a performing professional musician. He was born in East Moline, and he passed in East Moline. During his life, Pat Patrick ended up becoming a great baritone, alto, flute, tenor, bass, drum, piano, and clarinet player, writing, arranging, and directing lots of music. This alone qualifies him as a great American musician. There is plenty more of note.

Born Laurdine Patrick, he took on the nickname "Pat." His father was a musician also named Laurdine, and he had a devoted, church-singing and industrious mother named Lavern.

His parents moved to the Quad Cities—the adjacent and across-the-river cities of Rock Island, East Moline, and Moline, Illinois, plus Davenport,

19

Iowa—and then to Chicago as a part of that great exodus of Black families to the north, the great migrations where hundreds of thousands of Black folks landed in Chicago. All this happened in the early decades of the twentieth century. If you look simply at the images of Pat Patrick's family, you see all the indications of their place in the new decades ahead. They were "race people," that special brand of Black people born during the late nineteenth and early twentieth century who were imbued with all the promises, hopes, aspirations, and thinking given to them by generations of Black people who came before them. We remember the 1970s soul banner song, "Ain't No Stopping Us Now," and the images recall this sentiment. "The five years from 1924 into 1929 were no doubt the most prosperous ones the Negro community in Chicago had ever experienced. A professional and business class had arose upon the broad base of over seventy-five thousand colored wage earners and was able for a brief period to enjoy the first of its training and investment. . . . The fat years were at hand," so write the authors of the *Black Metropolis*, who help us to understand the air of Black potential of the period in Chicago for birthing and supporting the artistry of so many talented musicians from this period.[1] Pat Patrick was born into this. But not only him—there were many great musicians in Chicago during the 1960s and 1970s, several who were also Sun Ra's members. This period gave birth to an important musicians' movement in our nation's history, and that movement of ideas became embodied in the Association for the Advancement of Creative Musicians (AACM). Here again, these musicians were well trained by the same bandleader under whom Patrick studied, Captain Dyett at Dusable High School in Chicago. In music and arts, cultural context is everything. It establishes many of the parameters that define how a young artist not only sees him- or herself, but develops the legs to stand on to walk forward and claim the identity of artistry.

This explains the support mechanisms from the creative, cultural, and business sides. Dusable High was named after the city of Chicago's founder, Jean-Baptise Dusable. Dusable was a Haitian explorer-trader who lived from 1745 until 1818 and founded the first trading posts that would later develop into the city of Chicago. So we have a Black man founding a city, and there lands Pat Patrick. In this way, Chicago, particularly during this period, becomes a gift for our inquiry.

Clearly in his father's footsteps, Pat began at age four with dance and piano lessons. His father played in local bands, the same band as the famous, well-known trumpet great Clark Terry. (In fact, Terry lived in the Patrick home for a while.) Thus, Pat was influenced early on with this kind of musical presence as he began playing trumpet at nine.

Pat was twelve years old when his parents broke up, and his father moved to California.

Pat Patrick in High School
From the Pat Patrick Archive

Pat Patrick as a Young Professional
From the Pat Patrick Archive

Pat loved sports as well as music, but injured his hip playing football. He graduated from John Deere Junior High School in East Moline. But soon afterward, he and his mother, encouraged by Boston family members, moved to Boston, where he underwent hip surgery. The surgery required three months of recovery, then an additional eleven months in what was nearly a full body cast.

When he recovered, he and his mother moved to the suburbs of Chicago. By this time, he was interested in saxophone, and his mother purchased one for him. They learned of the famous Captain Walter Dyett, the bandleader at Dusable High School in Chicago. They moved into a neighborhood close to the high school so that Pat could attend. During Pat's time, Clifford Jordan, John Gilmore, Johnny Griffith, Julian Priester, Richard Davis, Richard Evans, and Ronnie Boykins were all students at Dusable, as well, and all would be involved in Pat's professional life in close ways.

Even in high school at age eighteen, Pat was an accomplished musician who was soon gigging at the Chicago Regal Theater, backing up Nat King Cole, Pearl Bailey, and others.

These Chicago roots are important because all great musicians refer to their "home soil"—who you are from a creative soil base, what you aspire to, and how that aspiration is of critical relevance. There was an important group of musicians who were all developing during this time in Chicago and their work had a tremendous impact on the future of American music styles, forms, and artistry.

This kind of "city music identity" can clearly be seen in other places, too, like in Detroit's Motown sound, Philadelphia's Philadelphia International Records, or Memphis's Stax Records.

In Indianapolis, a neighboring Midwestern community, there were during this same period neighborhoods, parks, and public schools where Black people were segregated in "good ways." Composer and bandleader Duke Ellington, coming up a generation earlier in Washington, D.C., even spoke of this as a plus, because it intensified pride. In those days, there were "race pride teachers" who felt it their duty to ensure youngsters would be equipped to be "better for the race."

These exchanges were in closed communities: in schools, churches, Black-owned barber shops. In Indianapolis in 1927, the Madame Walker Theater opened its doors to Blacks. Jazz composer, educator, trombonist David Baker, born in 1931, grew up in Indianapolis and attended the all-Black Crispus Attucks High School, which opened in 1927.

This is an example of great opportunities for the training of musicians who were taught by excellent teachers, many times by those who had advanced degrees and had been recruited from traditional Black colleges or from the army ranks, and the curricula included traditional music study as well as the study of contemporary music. These programs excelled in band literature and jazz, as well. The Indiana community, for example, included Baker, J. J. Johnson, Slide Hampton and family, and the Montgomery brothers, who were, again, all in public high schools. Indianapolis poet Mari Evans, quoted in David Baker's *Legacy in Music*, wrote,

> The neighborhood was sustaining. Children were protected and insulated by classrooms manned by Black teachers who cared passionately about their charges' futures, who saw promise in them, loved them, chastised them promptly, and encouraged them to be more than they envisioned. Those schools were places where Black children understood above all else they were loved, and being cared for with love.[2]

This is the context for learning despite the usual reports that public schools were lacking. Many musicians from both the South and North share similar stories about this period. This tells us a lot about how Pat Patrick and his Chicago colleagues were prepared early on and how they desired to see a world, a future for themselves in music, that was supported and nurtured. There is a lot of information about what these times provided for young musicians-in-training and then, later, for working musicians, and the evidence of these workings can be seen in the newspapers, playbills, clippings, and recordings. There is also, as we note from the Pat Patrick collection, a wealth of club postings that illustrate how live music thrived in the Chicago of the 1950s where Patrick performed. It is here that the foundation of his work ethic and "gigmanship" was formulated. This environment helped provide the essential experience that he needed to make the leap from Chicago to New York, where he settled in 1960.

THE YOUNG PROFESSIONAL MUSICIAN

Pat graduated from Dusable High in 1949 and was accepted on scholarship to Florida A&M University. But the South was not socially, racially, or musically conducive at the time, and Pat was not comfortable. So he returned to Chicago where he attended Wilson Junior College for two years. During these years of the early 1950s, his work as a player and local sideman in popular bands and orchestras began as he played behind Sammy Davis Jr., Nancy Wilson, Ernest Hawkins, and others.

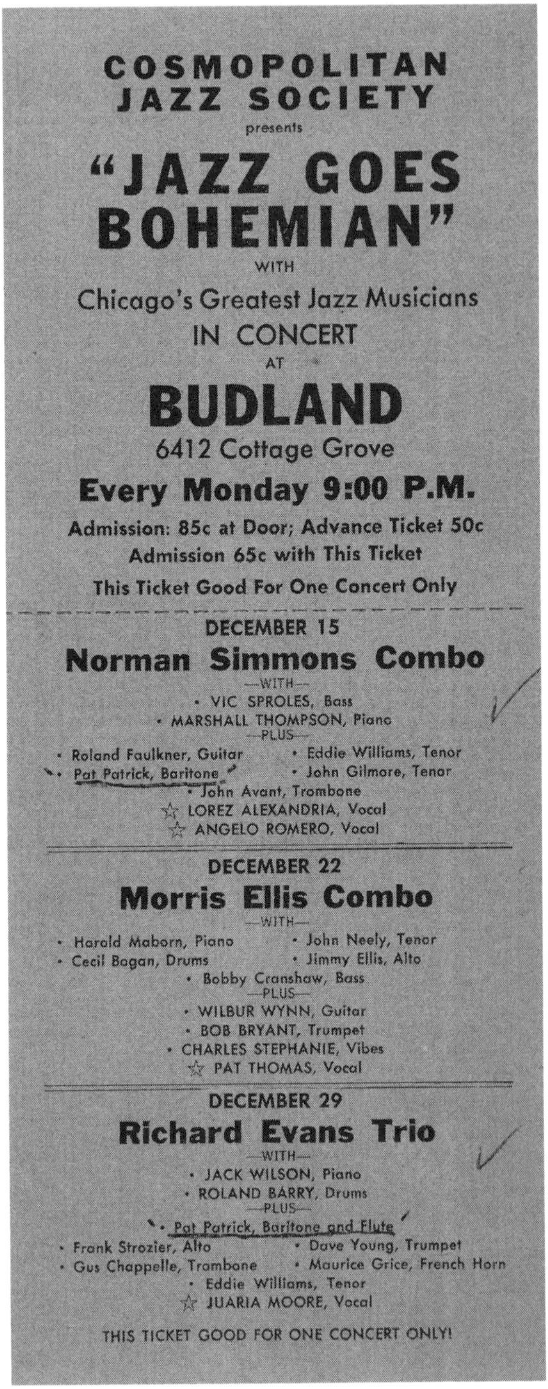

COSMOPOLITAN
JAZZ SOCIETY
presents
"JAZZ GOES
BOHEMIAN"
WITH
Chicago's Greatest Jazz Musicians
IN CONCERT
AT
BUDLAND
6412 Cottage Grove
Every Monday 9:00 P.M.
Admission: 85c at Door; Advance Ticket 50c
Admission 65c with This Ticket
This Ticket Good For One Concert Only

DECEMBER 15
Norman Simmons Combo
—WITH—
• VIC SPROLES, Bass
• MARSHALL THOMPSON, Piano
—PLUS—
• Roland Faulkner, Guitar
• Eddie Williams, Tenor
• Pat Patrick, Baritone
• John Gilmore, Tenor
• John Avant, Trombone
☆ LOREZ ALEXANDRIA, Vocal
☆ ANGELO ROMERO, Vocal

DECEMBER 22
Morris Ellis Combo
—WITH—
• Harold Maborn, Piano
• John Neely, Tenor
• Cecil Bogan, Drums
• Jimmy Ellis, Alto
• Bobby Cranshaw, Bass
—PLUS—
• WILBUR WYNN, Guitar
• BOB BRYANT, Trumpet
• CHARLES STEPHANIE, Vibes
☆ PAT THOMAS, Vocal

DECEMBER 29
Richard Evans Trio
—WITH—
• JACK WILSON, Piano
• ROLAND BARRY, Drums
—PLUS—
• Pat Patrick, Baritone and Flute
• Frank Strozier, Alto
• Dave Young, Trumpet
• Gus Chappelle, Trombone
• Maurice Grice, French Horn
• Eddie Williams, Tenor
☆ JUARIA MOORE, Vocal

THIS TICKET GOOD FOR ONE CONCERT ONLY!

Budland
From the Pat Patrick Archive

Then life began to open up. In 1954, Pat Patrick married Emily Winter Smith. Born from this marriage were Rhonda Patrick in 1955, then Deval Patrick in 1956. In 1954, Pat also made his first recording with Horace Henderson, brother of well-known band leader and composer Fletcher Henderson.

Around this time, in 1952, the dynamic musician Sonny Blount, soon to be known as Sun Ra, began assembling an early group he called the Space Trio. Pat Patrick joined as the second member after drummer Robert Barry. This early Sun Ra Space Trio made Pat the second original member of the soon-to-become famous Sun Ra Arkestra.

Soon other members joined the group, and Sun Ra began a regular stint at the Budland ballroom in Chicago. They began recording in 1956, and thus began the association that was to last three decades.

For Pat, an important recording session at this time involved being a sideman on the James Moody recording *Last Train from Overbrook* (Cadet Records). In 1959, a third Patrick child was born, La'Shon. In 1960, Pat was hired in the James Moody band, making important musical associations that would help him establish himself as a "first-call" player in the New York jazz community.

From his own resume, Pat shares,

> [I played] with Captain Walter Dyett, my high school band director, Illinois Jacquet, King Cole, Pearl Bailey, Louis Bellson, Budd DeFranco, Sil Auston, Muddy Waters, Cannonball Adderley, Roosevelt Sykes, Lil Armstrong, Dinah Washington, Della Reese, Erskine Hawkins, Cootie Williams, Eddie Haywood, Ahmad Jamal, Gene Ammons, Sun Ra, Johnny Griffin, Arthur Prysock, Jerry Butler, Bunny Briggs, Slappy White, Cab Calloway, [and] Dakota Staton.

In *A Power Stronger Than Itself*, George Lewis writes,

> Dusable High . . . opens its doors in the mid 1930s. [Band teacher] Dyett was celebrated far and wide for the pupils he nurtured to success in the music world. . . . Pianist Martha Davis, Dinah Washington, Nat "King" Cole, bassists Milt Hinton and Richard Davis . . . Dorothy Donegan . . . John Gilmore, all of these and more studied under Dyett. . . . Indeed, from the mid-1950s until his departure from Chicago in 1960, Sun Ra's work was a major aspect of Chicago's experimental musical atmosphere, and it would be reasonable to assume that his influence would have carried over to the younger generations.[3]

A very helpful account of Pat's early music life also is found in John F. Zwed's portrait of Sun Ra.

Pat Patrick as a Young Professional
From the Pat Patrick Archive

When [Pat] graduated from high school in 1949, he was awarded a scholarship to Florida A&M, but had returned to Chicago to enroll in Wilson Junior College. Patrick was something special, a musician of the right spirit, intelligent, honest, serious. . . . Patrick was the best musician Sonny had ever had in any of his bands. . . . The first step was to form the Space Trio. . . . Patrick on saxophones, a group which he [Sun Ra] saw as a vehicle to express his relationship to the world he knew and distrusted.[4]

While Pat Patrick's initial instruction as a musician came from his father, with further training occurring as he was mentored by teachers in school, he received serious tutoring from the many professionals with whom he worked, as was the tradition. When he was playing local gigs in Chicago before leaving for New York in the 1950s, he established himself as a player and bandleader. This prepared him for his years in New York and for his international performing career. These workings are shared throughout this book and include his

1. music gigs and dates;
2. recordings, both solo and those with other artists;
3. theater work as a musical director and arranger;

4. his baritone saxophone ensemble;
5. performances, tours, and recordings with Sun Ra;
6. radio shows and work as editor of *Black Theatre Magazine*;
7. composing and arranging; and
8. college teaching.

PROFESSIONAL CLIPPINGS

These numerous clippings are the first glimpse of Patrick's early Chicago professional life. It is illuminating to place these here from his archives as a part of his musical-life narrative.

July 1949
- With Otis Welch Orchestras, Bop City at Rose Bowl Ballroom, every Friday, beginning July 29, 1949
- The Regal, 1949 First Annual NAACP Midnight Show, one week in orchestra with Nat King Cole, Cootie Williams, Dinah Washington, and Illinois Jacket
- Big Progressive Club

September 15, 1950
- George Tolbert Review, Pat Patrick, Barry Sax
- Recordings on Chess Records

1951 Famous Door Sessions

1952 With Earl Fatha Hines, St. Louis, Missouri

1954
- With Horace Henderson, at New Trianon Ballroom, Chicago, South Side
- Horace Henderson and His Orchestra, June 24 and 26, 1954; 62nd Street and Cottage Grove Avenue, Cottage Grove
- Recorded with Horace Henderson, July 10, 1954, Chicago, WIND broadcast, at Trianon Ballroom, July 17 and July 24

January 30, 1955
- Pat Patrick and His All Stars
- Carven High School B Auditorium

Earl Hines Orchestra: Kiez Auditorium, April 1952
From the Pat Patrick Archive

1956

- January 1956 recorded with Billie Hawkins and the Sun Ra Orchestra, Chicago, Heartbeat Recordings
- February, April, and May 1956 recorded with Sun Ra and His Arkestra, Saturn Recordings
- October 1956 recorded with Andrew Hill Combo, Chicago, Ping Recordings #1003, recorded "Down Pat," Patrick composition. This piece became a well-known swinging recording on jukeboxes. The Ping Record 45 lists "'Down Pat' (L. Patrick), featuring L. Patrick"

1958

- December 20, 1958, in the *Chicago Defender*: "'Monday Jazz Sessions at the Budland,' Chicago's top jazz recording artists and vocalists will be featured . . . such well known artists as . . . Pat Patrick, John Gilmore"
- September 7, 8, and 19 recorded with James Moody, Chicago, *Last Train from Overbrook*, Cadet Recordings

1959
- *The Cry of Jazz* film is released, featuring the Sun Ra Arkestra
- December 29, Cosmopolitan Jazz Society, at Budland, with Pat Patrick, John Gilmore, and Richard Evans

As Charles Davis explains in an interview about Pat Patrick, "Pat Patrick was a hell of a musician, composer, creator. I remember in the Chicago days there was a hit of his they used to play on the jukeboxes. It was called 'Down Pat,' on Ping Records, I believe. It was a D♭ flat Blues, this was in the 1950s. He was dedicated" (see chapter 9 for more of Davis's interview).

"DOWN PAT"

This piece is the earliest recording that captures in an important way what was "to become." It is the first example of Pat Patrick's commercial work as a young, active musician in Chicago, at twenty-seven years old. He is paired here with one of the early leading jazz thinkers, Chicago-born composer and pianist Andrew Hill. Hill, like Patrick, Sun Ra, and others, would leave shortly to land in New York, further extending the Chicago roots eastward. Patrick would rejoin Hill in recording again on January 16, 1970, in New York at Bluenote, where he also recorded with Charles Tolliver, Bennie Maupin, Ron Cater, and Paul Motian. This 1956 collaboration for Patrick was equally a musical triumph because it features both his composition and his stellar playing— a signature opening lick of the record with the baritone saxophone. That great sound and performance would be mirrored throughout the industry in the 1960s with baritone sax–led breaks in rock-and-roll and pop songs. This lick was an antecedent to Sun Ra's later hit in 1970, *Space Is the Place*, which also opens with a baritone sax signature intro lick played by Danny Thompson.

It's easy here to imagine the dual impact of this recording because it's Pat's playing and his composition. This set him in motion in many ways in the industry as a player and writer early on. The musician's axe (instrument) is always his or her best imprint onto—and cut into—music, and the identity of the baritone saxophone as a "sound" gets further carried on with both Charles Davis and Pat Patrick, who twenty years later form the Baritone Saxophone Retinue (described as "a new sound on the scene"), a historic group consisting of only baritone saxophones. This was pathbreaking.

Quite another aspect of this now-classic recording is the virtuosity of Pat Patrick's deft performance. This is the mark of his great musicianship as a player that won him quick entry into his forthcoming recording and gigging years in New York.

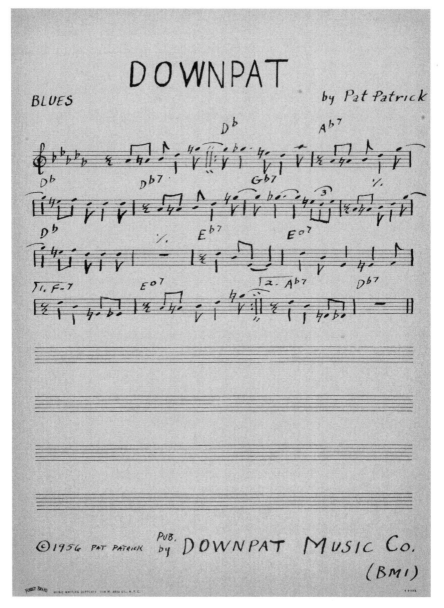

"Down Pat," 1956
From the Pat Patrick Archive

Pat Patrick "outsessioned" most of his contemporaries during the early 1960s, playing, some weeks, a session every other day with some of the biggest jazz names in the business, including James Moody, Quincy Jones, Mongo Santamaria, and John Coltrane. From this 1956 beginning, those recording dates would grow from a modest showing of 105 record dates on other artists' albums during the 1960s to thirty-eight record albums in the 1970s to six in the 1980s, totaling more than 150 record dates.

THE CRY OF JAZZ (1959)

At the very opening of the 1959 film *The Cry of Jazz*, a principal character states, "Jazz is dead; it no longer matters." Although this may be easier to state today, it was difficult to claim in the 1950s, because for many, jazz music and culture loomed larger than life. Jazz was the quintessential musical expression of what life meant to many young musicians and fans. As is noted later, thousands of young musicians moved upward and outward into maturity and into society through the performance of the music. For many Americans, jazz also represented a "sound of accomplishment and artistry." Nat King Cole's "Pick Yourself Up"—so "take a deep breath, pick yourself up, dust yourself off, and start all over again"—from his 1962 recording is a primary example.

In short, jazz was the popular music of the day, soon to be replaced by rock-and-roll, which would emerge in 1957. But in the 1950s, jazz was the frame through which contemporary culture was expressed for young musicians. As for beboppers, the big debates of race, creativity, and social design could be seen. For Duke Ellington, the statement of essential meaning was "It don't mean a thing if it ain't got that swing," and for Charley Parker, it was "Music is your own experience, your own thoughts, your wisdom. If you don't live it, it won't come out of your horn. They teach you there's a boundary line to music. But, man, there's no boundary line to art."[5] Later, John Coltrane stated, "I think the main thing a musician would like to do, is give a picture to the listener of the many wonderful things he knows and senses in the universe. That's what music is to me."[6] Contemporary performer and composer Dr. Ysaye Barnwell of Sweet Honey in the Rock stated it this way:

> It is clear to me from looking from an African world view that music exists because it does something. It never is the art for art's sake kind of phenomenon. If it doesn't make it rain, if it doesn't infuse herbs with a healing spirit, then what good is a song? Quincy Jones asks, "What good is a song if it doesn't inspire, if it has no message to bring? If a song doesn't take you

E VEN FOR the abundant brain power of a novelist, housing analyst, mathematician and serious music composer the idea of forming a Negro movie company was at once ambitious and audacious. Messrs. Mark Kennedy, Nelam L. Hill, Eugene Titus and Edward O. Bland,

Film company heads Edward O. Bland, Eugene Titus, Nelam L. Hill and Mark Kennedy plan series defining the Negro in U. S.

52

Ed Bland, *Cry of Jazz*
From the Pat Patrick Archive

higher, higher, higher, what good is it to sing?" We can see how our music has evolved and at every point that our history has taken another turn, our music has taken another turn. That is evidence of music's functionality. Then when you start to look at what the music says and how it was created and how it is used, it is totally clear that we have never dropped that aspect of who we are as African people.[7]

The Cry of Jazz, created by Edward O. Bland, a young Chicago-area DJ who was an advocate of the music and interested in the importance and creation of Black music, played Sun Ra's music on the radio and was a huge supporter. He asked Sun Ra to provide the movie soundtrack. Bland actually used the Sun Ra band not only to provide a musical backdrop, but he placed the performing orchestra in the film. In this way, the film became a sort of early Sun Ra music video. There were many other examples of this; for example, the 1929 film short of Bessie Smith in *St. Louis Blues*, the Duke Ellington band's appearances in the 1930 *Check and Double Check* movie, and the 1943 *Cabin in the Sky*, as well as Lena Horn, Cab Calloway, and Fatts Waller in *Stormy Weather*, also in 1943.

Besides the visual identity of a talented Black band, *The Cry of Jazz* explores the relationship between jazz and the Black music tradition, accompanying and representing the sociopsychological condition and expression of Black and white people in America. Sonny Blount—Sun Ra—was a man who had, up until this time at age thirty-eight, spent a lot of time thinking about and dedicating his work to some of these social/cultural issues in many ways. He would find very different answers but brought along a group of younger musicians through which the expression of the music addressed social ideas more forwardly than in previous big bands and ensembles. Pat Patrick was a critical member of that mix. The film's opening questions, raised first by a young white woman, are answered by engaged and informed young Black men, friends who state, "Jazz is the cry of the Negroes," "joy and suffering," but also the "expression of the triumph of the Negro spirit." They also state, "The Negro is the only true 'human American.'" Not far from these arguments, although a much more complex one, is Ralph Ellison's *The Invisible Man* and, more recently, Albert Murray's concept of Blacks as the "Omni American."

Bland's film represents the 1950s as a most satisfying attempt to pose and engage the question of racial-cultural formulas presented in authentic expression and, in this case especially, the most-talked-about music of the day, jazz. Prophetically, the film raises these questions not far from the near–cultural onslaught of rock-and-roll and soul music traditions of the 1960s.

The question of aesthetics—purposeful writing addressing social identity through the engagement of art and culture—looms huge in the Ra workings.

This additionally addressed the questions about the technical sound of the band. It's upon hearing the soundtrack that you note a clear grounding in bebop and the seriousness of focused musicianship and high-quality performance of this early pre–New York band of 1956 to 1960.

What's striking about the film is the sophistication of the arguments framed not only in social, class, and racial questions, but in holding close to musical forms, structures, definitions of what is termed "constrictions of individuality, release, abandon, restraint, expression, improvisation, emotion, intellectualism, existentialism, gestures, walk and dance, present-moment, conflict, sonority and sound, then, and harmony and stress." *The Cry of Jazz* then utilizes this with a biting critique of American social racial casting as the realization of the futureless future. Further, the film presents jazz music as the global expression of the "existence on the definition of the present" and acts in culture as a "super-thought of forwardness."

The film piece is a sophisticated social framing, a visual display of Black life in the 1950s, which shows Blacks in diverse cultural situations in pool halls, out dining, in communities, attending sophisticated jazz concerts, in neighborhoods and various settings where people are displayed as normal, everyday living Americans. It is also a great picture of Black Americans shot through the lens of everyday folks in Chicago, equally important in understanding Patrick's life setting as a young musician.

Additionally, the film is a major link in Pat's story, as it also answers a series of questions about the look and sound of Sun Ra's Chicago band in performance. The film features prominently a young Pat Patrick seen in solo performances in 1956 and 1957, during the prime of his early professional life in Chicago. The film makes the clear argument for the humanization of America through Black music experience and posits that America could learn and gain its value through the Negro, Negro expression, and its salvific experience. More wonderfully and valuable is the clear argument for the value of jazz as a social sounding of cultural relevance. As one character states, "Without the existence of jazz, there would certainly be no Negro human soul, and if no Negro human soul presented, a very diminished America."

This relates very clearly to Patrick's essay from 1973, as he states,

> To improve on this [race] situation, is a monumental task that only true art and artists can accomplish. . . . At this time there is a definite need for Black people to know and understand, appreciate their own culture, to be able to recognize, desire it and not be ashamed of it in this environment we live, exist in, lest our own unique identity dwindle and disappear. We must be aware that our hearing is not dulled by the drone of meaningless music. With all this, you might raise the question: Where is real music? Where can it be found and how does it sound? I would offer as a suggestion to try Sun Ra Arkestra.

And so this view from the early Patrick days in Chicago offers a glimpse into what begins to shape his artistry and worldview. This will become a lifeline for many Americans by the 1970s, and the main theme for most of the music from this period.

At the same time, the theme of family is addressed in many ways. The Sun Ra band actually holds its practice sessions in Pat Patrick's mother's home during this time. Now married with two young children, Pat felt his loyalties split here—being a devoted father and a devoted musician within a strong family "apparatus." The pull of the Sun Ra band begs the questions raised earlier regarding what forces were pulling at this highly creative musician in this musician-driven environment, what sacrifices were being made, and what costs to defining what it meant to be a musician in the decade ahead.

INTERVIEW WITH PAT'S HIGH SCHOOL FRIEND JEAN L. MCKINNEY

Bill Banfield: Jean, tell me about Pat during your high school years at Dusable. What was he like as a young man?

Jean Mckinney: Well, I went to high school and graduated with him. Pat was a loner; he didn't hang. He just liked to play his horn. When we were around, he was a real nonchalant person, somebody we would call a "hip square." That's a really old term. You know you are square in your demeanor, but you are really trying to be hip. And that was really him, you know. He wasn't loud or fast talking, he was always cool and into himself, quiet. We had a nickname and used to call him "liver lips." Because he had them big juicy lips, you know. He used to just laugh and say, "Well, those are my chops so don't say anything about them." He was the typical acting, looking young musician of those days.

Bill Banfield: Were you aware of the other musicians he was around as a young player?

Jean Mckinney: Yes, I was, because I had a jump on this. I danced in a thing called High Jinx. I took dancing from the Egerton Dancing School. I was therefore able to know some of the musicians: Paul Sorano, Paul Gussman, although not Nat Cole's group. They were a little older. A guy we used to call Boot; the local musicians. I was sort of outgoing, that's what made Pat laugh at me all the time. Pat was just cool and loved to play his horn. You never saw him without it. I can't ever remember him being without his horn. We used to dance at a couple places he would play. Bacon's Casino, on 49th and Wabash, was a place he played, catty-corner from Dusable. A lot of the bands would play there. My girlfriend's name was Joan, and I was Jean. They used to call us Jean and Joan. We got a kick out of that. We had a great time. Pat had a band himself.

In 1958, he played at Gerri's Palm Garden, that was a real nice place up on 47th Street, right off of South Park. He played and sang. In those days, everybody was trying to sing like Billy Eckstine. He was playing and singing. I knew some of the guys who played in the band—Earl Ezell and Kip King, who died recently; Clifton Major. They all grew up in the Dusable band together. There was a guy named Calvin Latner; all these people are dead now, baby.

Bill Banfield: Tell me about growing up in the 1940s, 1950s, living in Chicago.

Jean Mckinney: In those days, I tried to make all the dances and be around all the musicians. The Regal Theater was one of the most exciting places we could go. And the places on the south side. We went to the Savoy. There was a lot of skating during that time. We went downtown. I graduated at eighteen in 1949. As quiet as it's kept, we loved Benny Goodman. I liked Duke Ellington when his bands came through. In 1949, 1950, I didn't see us as progressive enough. If you didn't go to college, you weren't going to do anything. We went to community college, business college, and tried to get jobs.

I got married, had children, got good jobs; that was my group growing up in Chicago.

All this you telling me. I didn't know Pat had become a famous musician. Somebody told me that they heard of him being broadcast playing in a club in the 1980s. Nobody from that time is alive now. But I never knew he became really known as a musician!

Artistry, New York 1960–1969

So I had the very distinct pleasure of playing with people like
Nat Cole, Don Redman, Illinois Jacket, Cootie Williams, Pearl
Bailey, Eartha Kitt, Sammy Davis Jr., Redd Foxx, Flip Wilson,
any number of dynamite people. Not to mention the people who
were still in Chicago at the time like King Collax, Gene Ammonds, Johnny Griffin, all those giants around town. . . . Chicago
at that time was on the ebb of what was at that time one of the
greatest musical episodes in the history of African American
music that there has probably ever been.

—Pat Patrick, from a radio interview

My most vivid memory of my father centers on the day he left.
. . . I didn't know for many years why my father left. All I knew
was that he had moved to New York with his band, the Sun Ra
Arkestra.

—Deval Patrick, *A Reason to Believe*

$\mathcal{S}$un Ra, the man who wrote about the future, moved his stellar band from
Chicago to New York in 1960. He and his brand of musicianship had come
to take us into the future toward the mysteries that had been revealed to

him. For Pat Patrick, the arrival to New York brought a different yet related reality to his professional aspirations. Unlike Sun Ra, who maintained his single-mindedness and devotion to building the meaning of his work and ideas through the Sun Ra Arkestra, Pat Patrick, once in New York, could more fully realize his aspirations as a full-fledged working musician in the world's leading performing town—the Big (gig) Apple. Word spread fast, and contacts and calls propelled his talent and hardworking drive.

His supreme ability and aspiration as a musician allowed him to break away and rise above so many other talented Ra musicians. In Patrick, we sense a musical achiever who was destined to draw lots of attention. He received many calls.

During the 1960s, Pat Patrick can be seen performing on more than one hundred albums with the leading jazz artists in New York, as well as performing in working ensembles. At the same time, he worked as an arranger, bandleader, and musical director for Mongo Santamaria, Michael Olatunji's Afro-American Dance Company, and many theater productions.

THE 1960s

During these early New York years, Patrick played with other leading musician-led bands, such as those of Johnny Griffith, Jimmy Heath, John Coltrane, Cootie Williams, Russell Procope, Duke Ellington, and Quincy Jones. This working focus expands from musicianship to leadership to global citizenship. International performances would accompany this growth, as Patrick performed in Germany, Egypt, Italy, and Switzerland. It was during these years that the critical creative association with Nigerian playwright Wole Sonyinka flowered into a series of theatrical works in which Pat wrote the music and served as music director.

Pat Patrick writes from his resume,

- Recorded with Sun Ra, James Moody, Jimmy Heath, Blue Mitchell, Frank Strozier, Cannonball Adderley and Ernie Wilkens, Quincy Jones, Olatunji, Mongo Santamaria, Louis Ramirez, Pete Bonet, A. K. Salim, Phil Upchurch, Freddy Mccoy, Andrew Hill, John Coltrane, and a Maxwell House Coffee TV commercial with Geoffrey Holder
- Compositions recorded: "Mambo Village," recorded by Johnny Zamont, Mongo Santamaria; "Quiet Stroll," "Yeh Yeh," "Nothing for Nothing," "The Boogie Can Blues Main," "Not Hardy," by Mongo Santamaria, "Yeh Yeh," a #1 hit in England by Georgia Fame, Lambert Hendricks and Bayanm, "The 3 Sounds" by Gerald Wilson, Hollywood Brass, Ferry Fielding, Baby Cortez, Jon Hendricks, and Frank Porcel; "Latino

Baby," "Catfish Bag," "Gaboon," recorded by Johnny Zamont; "A Tune for The Tudor," Coleman Hawkins, Clark Terry
- 1960 to 1961 worked with James Moody Septet, Worlds Fair (NYC)
- Recorded with Johnny Griffith, The Big-Soul Johnny Griffin Orchestra with Clark Terry, Pat Patrick, Charles Davis, Julien Priester (TB), May 24, 31, June, 3, 1960, New York, Riverside Recordings
- Recorded with Jimmy Heath, Really Big! Jimmy Health Orchestra, June 24, 28, 1960, New York
- Recorded with John Coltrane, Africa Brass
- John Coltrane Quartet, Englewood Cliffs, May 23, 1961, New Jersey, Impulse Recordings
- Duke Ellington, 1961
- Quincy Jones' Orchestra, Live at Newport, July 3, 1961, Newport, Rhode Island
- Recorded with Frank Stokier Quartet, September 12, 1961, New York, Jazzland Recordings
- Phil Diaz, Cal Jader, Mongo Santamaria ("Watermelon Man"), New York, December 17, 1962, recording
- Performed with Clarke Terry, Coleman Hawkins, Lambert and Hendricks
- Recorded (multiple) with Sun Ra Arkestra, October 1961, 1962, New York, Savoy, Saturn Recordings
- Recorded with Mongo Santamaria, Live the Black Hawk, San Francisco, California, 1962
- Recorded with Cannonball Adderley and His Orchestra, New York, June 25, 1962, Riverside Recordings
- Recorded with Mongo Santamaria, Go Mongo, July, 9, 11, 1962, New York, Milestone Recordings
- Recorded with Sam Jones, August 15, 1961, New York, Riverside Recordings
- Recordings with Sun Ra Arkestra 1962–1969 (multiple)
- Recorded with Mongo Santamaria, "Watermelon Man," December 17, 1962, New York, Milestone Recordings
- Recorded with Mongo Santamaria, February 18, 19, 1963, New York [Mongo Records, includes Patrick's "Yeh Yeh," which later becomes a hit]
- Recorded with Mongo Santamaria, Mongo at Village Gate, Spring 1964, New York
- Recorded with A. K. Salim, Afro Soul Drum Orgy, October, 8, 1964, New York
- Recorded with Pharoah Sanders and Black Harold, December 31, 1964, New York, Saturn Recordings
- Served as music director for Afro-American Dance Group
- Performed in the New York World's Fair with Babatunde Olatunji, African Pavilion
- 1965 touring colleges with Sun Ra

MUSIC AND FAMILY

One of the themes mentioned in the opening of this book is Patrick's challenge and conflict: pursuing the life of a professional musician while balancing family life. This is one of the benchmark issues of artists across the spectrum, many of whom are torn by the life, the drive, drama, and pull of professional artistry and are challenged to meet family commitments. The emotional, psychological, and physical drain has many times created counterproductive actions.

In music, you hear of the broken club dates, the dives, the gigging, one-nighters, performing from town to town, and the rejections. For someone like Patrick, who was not the famous lead but the sideman, the constant nomadic life of the working musician is a story that goes untold.

Patrick's face may not have been on the TV, but his work and voice were prominently heard through his prolific playing, which touched many recordings and ensembles as evidenced in the listing above. Managing this schedule and his family life was challenging. This challenge played a role in his ideas and music and in the role he saw for himself as a "light bearer," a term he uses in his papers. One of the challenges was the strained and then realigned relationship with his son, former Massachusetts governor, Deval Patrick. In his memoir, *A Reason to Believe*, Deval Patrick provides a riveting account of his own struggle to come to grips with his "absent" father who left home to pursue his music. Deval Patrick tells the most beautiful of estranged-father-and-son stories in a chapter entitled "Save a Place."

He writes, "Nothing had been settled, but it was the beginning of a process in which I would try to forgive him for the hurt his long absence had caused us, and he would try to accept me for the man I was becoming. I would save a place."[1]

The theme of acceptance and forgiveness as a process of redemption makes this chapter a powerful and beautiful telling of a father and son relationship in healing. Because this pulls to the realistic center of the Pat Patrick story, a deeper dissonance of relationships rings out through the musician's music and workings. As his daughter La'Shon noted, "He has all these bonds, but estranged amongst his family. I don't know what happened to him."

Deval Patrick further writes in *A Reason to Believe*, "I also felt disappointment and anger and a certain amount of shame in having an absentee father, though that was not uncommon on the south side. . . . He blew sax, which the other kids thought was cool."[2]

When Pat left Chicago for New York in 1960, he left his family behind. His wife Emily did not want to move to New York, was devastated by the breakup, and never remarried. Deval Patrick writes that this "started her on a long slide into bitterness and depression."[3] Though Deval, in the ensuing years, would spend time with both parents, this marital break became one of life's bitter pages between Pat Patrick and him, and that page stayed present and opened until the end of Pat's life. As son Deval writes again in his biography, "My father's love for music, which brought joy to so many, led to disaster" for the family.[4]

As a gigging musician, Patrick also avoided his financial responsibilities to take care of his children and wife. It was not until Deval was a senior at his beloved Milton High School outside of Boston that he was told by his grandfather one reason why Pat left the family: he had fathered another child while away from home. Rhonda and Deval's half sister, La'Shon Anthony, was born in Chicago in 1959. This helps shed light on a growing life difficulty with his broken family situation in Chicago, complicated now by not only by professional aspirations in music but the personal challenges of being responsible for three young children with two different mothers. Pat's own demons, estrangement from family, and a growing sociopolitical rage against the system led to harsh relations with his son. New York must have also been a kind of hiding place for him.

Patrick Children in Chicago
From the Pat Patrick Archive

Rhonda Patrick
From the Pat Patrick Archive

Pat Patrick Playing Chess with Deval
From the Pat Patrick Archive

La'Shon Anthony
From the Pat Patrick Archive

La'Shon Anthony
From the Pat Patrick Archive

Rhonda and Deval Patrick
From the Pat Patrick Archive

INTERVIEW WITH RHONDA PATRICK-SIGH

We spoke to Pat's daughter, Rhonda Patrick-Sigh, on April 5, 2014. We talked about her early days growing up in Chicago, visiting Pat in the summers with her brother Deval during the 1970s, traveling on the road with the Sun Ra band, the process of rehearsals, the respect the members had for their leader, the organization of the rehearsals and performances, and then Pat Patrick's last days.

Rhonda Patrick-Sigh: I was remembering a time when I was really young, maybe about three, and we were at the dinner table in Chicago. We were living in a basement apartment on 79th and Calumet. I must have been acting up at the table. I don't remember him spanking me or physical punishment. But this one time I was acting up and instead of spanking me, he took my cup of milk and poured it over my head. And of course it's cold; I'm in shock, and I am trying to catch my breath. But it got my attention! And that was his way, which was so like him, he's so different. Who does that? It did the trick—that was his unique way of disciplining me.

There were times when he would stop talking to me when he was upset. There were times, too, where he spaced out during the time he and my mother were separating. One time that stands out to me was in 1964. My brother, Deval, and I flew by ourselves to be with him in New York for the summer. That was his gig for the summer, working with Olantunji at the African Pavilion at the World's Fair. And that was amazing. I remember the dancers and the family; the band members. We used to spend every day, night, in the Pavilion, which was made up of these huts from all over the world. So we were learning, too, and by the end of the summer we knew all the dance moves. It was so much fun. Just being there in the atmosphere, like visiting all the countries, cultures. For us at age eight, nine, that was pretty incredible.

My mother put me in dance classes at age three. So I aspired to be a dancer since then.

So this further propelled my desire to dance even more.

It was a real family. I remember one of the dancers, Sheryl, had my ears pierced for the first time. The dancers were like my aunts. It was a great experience.

There were other times that we made these visits to New York. Dad brought us. He was always, always doing gigs here and there. He lived in a one-room apartment in the Bronx then. I remember him teaching us the culture of New York and how fast paced it was. I remember him taking us on the train and him showing me how to stand on the train while it's moving, how to balance and the move of the train. I still try and do that today and taught my kids how to do it. Running around to different places; music stores.

In high school I had a boyfriend, so I don't remember a lot of time with Pat in those years. Later on when I was twenty-one, I was in the Sun Ra band, dancing. I went on the 1976/1977 European tour. I believe it was when I graduated from beauty school. My graduation gift from Pat was to take me to Europe.

But the way he could do it was to enlist me as a dancer in the band, which was correct because I was a trained dancer. So we left in June, headed to Paris. We were staying in a small hotel. It was set up as our home base, going back and forth to other countries, a gig or two out, but then we always came back to Paris. Holland, then to Switzerland, three cites in Italy, Rome, Milan, then to Nice, the French Rivera.

I was always scared of Sun Ra then. Just his presence. He had a very serious demeanor that was very large, a larger-than-life kind of personality. I was very shy. He was very serious, very deep. Everything that came out of his mouth, you had to really think about it. He wasn't a jokester, so I kind of stayed out of his way.

Of course you learn when you get older, actually he was the one I should have been spending more time with because he was so deep and had these wise thoughts.

I was close to June Tyson. She was the mother of the group. She had her daughter there who was younger than me. But she put herself in the mother role.

With the dancing that I remember, well, there must have been some kind of rehearsal, but I never saw a strict rehearsal. It was all, well, like free dance, modern self-expression, like free jazz. It was just the "move of the spirit." During a show, it's whenever I felt ready. I just came out and danced. There wasn't any strict routine; it wasn't like that, when you felt ready, you danced; self-expression. The two other dancers would dance together but still not synchronized.

The band was like that too. They were together. They had their rhythm, but they all had self-expression.

They were all very respectful of Sun Ra, and they thought the world of him. There was no jive, all business. They knew this was serous. It wasn't just playing music, but it was a movement. Everybody took it seriously, and they had great relationships, no fights, never anything like having serious disagreements and different views that were upsetting. They all got along. It was really like a family. We were on the road for two months that year.

I was trying to understand him [Sun Ra]. And that's one thing I can appreciate from Pat. My dad really exposed me to Sun Ra and the music. I actually heard him in Chicago, before this time. I thought the music was, "He has lost his mind! What in the heck?" I said, "Wow, that's different."

I had no idea that my dad was working on this all the time he was in New York. I didn't understand it. I didn't know what to say. But when I traveled with them, my eyes were opened up to a whole new understanding of this kind of music. And I think it came with hanging out with them and understanding them, their personalities, coming out in the music, which to me is more genuine, and more meaningful than, say, just playing some chords that are laid out. But to have their personalities come out in the music? To me, that's what it is all about. I said, "I get it."

1966–1969

Pat Patrick writes from his resume,

> [I played] brief periods with Montego Joe, Machito, Marvin Gaye, Kim Weston, Marvelettes, Billy Taylor, Chuck Jackson, Kako Ysu, Patty Labelle and the Blue Bells, numerous colleges of the East and West Coast with Sun Ra and two days of concerts at Carnegie Hall, the Jean-Leon Destine Haitian Dance Company, the Nigerian Highlife Orchestras, composed music for plays by Nigerian playwright Wole Soyinka [*The Strange Breed*, Greenwich Village, New York, October 1967], *Kongi's Harvest*, produced by the Negro Ensemble Company, 1968, D.C. I was a disc jockey on WBAI-FM radio, doing shows on roots of jazz, the music of Sun Ra.

The Wole Soyinka Theater Run

A review in *New York Free Press* in 1967 reports this about Wole Soyinka's plays:

> The polarity that has been created by the terms of categorization, between African music and American music, is being bridged with a culture lifeline, initiated by the active participation and working together of African and American artists. . . . The music from these plays, composed and arranged by Pat Patrick, fills in and creates the strong and natural environment needed to put the play across . . . the blending of the sounds, presented as sound values related to the words . . . feeling, sounds of flutes and drums provides a live screen on which the play comes alive.

One of the most interesting and widely documented of Pat's creative periods came between 1967 and 1968, when he worked on Wole Soyinka's plays: *The Trial of Brother Jero*, *The Strong Breed*, and *Kongi's Harvest*. A promotional advertisement reads, "The first big hit of the season, the critics all agree."

The New York Times, Village Voice, New Yorker Magazine, Cue Magazine, Daily News, Humm Variety, New York Post, Wall Street Journal,

Jersey Journal, New York Evening News, Westside News, Free Press, and *Time Magazine* all wrote enthusiastically about these works. *Village Voice,* in November 23, 1967, reported, "The music and sound by Pat Patrick are enormously helpful . . . worth a visit for their entertaining freshness and direct theatricality."

The music of these productions was promoted on all advertisements, posters, programs, and flyers. It was essential to the drama and received top billing. It was not simply the score or "musical underbed." It was integral to the story. On each of the publicity posters, directly under the title, you see the name of the playwright Wole Soyinka, as well as "music by Pat Patrick." BMI music, a major publishing company in a piece titled "The Many Worlds of Music," noted,

> Following the success earlier this season of Wole Soyinka's *The Trial of Brother Jero* and *The Strong Breed,* the Negro Ensemble Company presented *Kongi's Harvest,* another work by the Nigerian playwright, at New York's St. Mark's playhouse. . . . The play deals with the fall of a dictator who rules an emergent African nation. Directed by Michael A. Schultz, the music for the satiric drama, was written by Pat Patrick.

With the 1968 production of *Kongi's Harvest, Amsterdam News* critic Raymond Robinson's characterization noted, "Ensemble's New Work Exciting. . . . The production, in a frighteningly ceremonial dance number erupts. . . . The choreography is quite good and sets a pace that continues to [the] end. . . . The entire cast (and crew) can be credited with an exciting and absorbing production."

What's of note here is the absence of the playwright Wole Soyinka himself. He certainly is well known and highly regarded during this period. These African play debuts were "a first," the first time a major African playwright was produced to critical acclaim in New York. Yet during this time, Mr. Soyinka was in prison in Nigeria, accused of working for Nigerian independence. In *Kongi's Harvest,* the central character is a self-declared "prophet of God," an educated hero who is chosen by the villagers to perform a traditional ceremony and who is then faced with the challenge of being modern while also heeding tradition's call. Soyinka was clearly aware that his work would sit in the global context telling Nigeria's story, but also reflecting America's social revolution. As *Time* magazine stated in April 26, 1968, "Soyinka's voice is being heard loud and clear off Broadway. . . . There is interest in seeing how an African writes about turning tribes into nations."

t week in "Kongi's   Raysor, Maxine Griffith,
at the St. Mark's   Robert Hooks and Denise
. In the cast are,   Nicholas.

THE NEW YORK TIMES, TUESDAY, MARCH 26, 1968

DOUGLAS TURNER WARD, *Artistic Director*

ROBERT HOOKS, *Executive Director*

GERALD S. KRONE, *Administrative Director*

The Company:

Norman Bush
Rosalind Cash
David Downing
Francis Foster
Arthur French
Moses Gunn
William Jay
Judyann Jonsson
Denise Nicholas
Esther Rolle
Clarice Taylor
Hattie Winston
Allie Woods

Edmund Cambridge,
   Production Stage Manager

the Negro Ensemble Company

APRIL 9 – MAY 12

KONGI'S HARVEST

by WOLE SOYINKA

Directed by Michael A. Schultz
Dance Direction by Louis Johnson
Sets by Edward Burbridge
Costumes by Jeanne Button
Lighting by Jules Fisher
— *Music by Pat Patrick* —

PREVIEWS APRIL 4 thru 7. ALL SEATS $3.00

MAIL & PHONE ORDERS: Tues., Wed., Thurs. 8:30, Sun. 3 & 8:30: $4.50, 3.50,
Fri. 8:30, Sat. 7 & 10:30: $4.95, 3.95. Please enclose self-addressed stamped enve-
lope. List 3 alternate dates. Make checks payable to Negro Ensemble Company.

ST. MARKS PLAYHOUSE, 133 2nd AVE. (8th ST.) OR 4-3530

Kongi's Harvest, Sole-Patrick Collaboration
From the Pat Patrick Archive

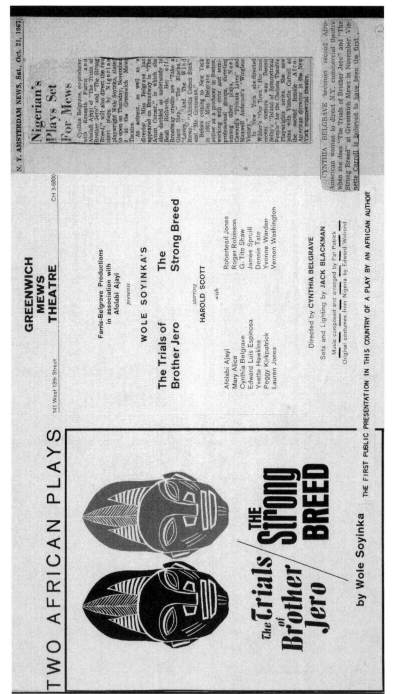

The Trials of Brother Jero/Strong Breed, Sole-Patrick Collaboration
From the Pat Patrick Archive

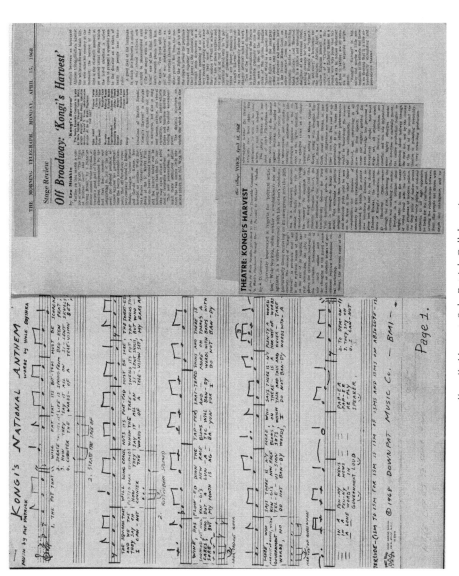

Kongi's Harvest, Sole-Patrick Collaboration
From the Pat Patrick Archive

THE MORNING TELEGRAPH, MONDAY, APRIL 15, 1968

Stage Review

Off Broadway: 'Kongi's Harvest'

by Leo Mishkin

Earlier on this season a couple of one-act plays, "The Trials of Brother Jero" and "The Strong Breed," by a Nigerian author named Wole Soyinka, attracted a good deal of favorable attention, compounded by the fact that their creator was languishing in jail at the moment for alleged political offenses against his government. Now the Negro Ensemble Company, that off-Broadway repertory company headed by Robert Hooks, Douglas Turner Ward and Gerald S. Krone, has brought us another Wole Soyinka drama, "Kongi's Harvest," down at the St. Marks Playhouse on lower Second Avenue, and the verdict today can be nothing else than that Mr. Soyinka may again attract a good deal of favorable attention.

This new presentation is a much more ambitious effort than the two simple little one-acters shown last fall. With in-

'Kongi's Harvest'

The Negro Ensemble Company is a play by Wole Soyinka, Douglas Turner Ward, artistic director; Robert Hooks, executive director; Gerald S. Krone, administrative director. At the St. Marks Playhouse.

THE CAST

Ogbo Aweri	Frances Foster
Sarumi	Clarice Taylor
Ogbo Aweri	Frances Foster
	Rosalind Cash
Wuraola	Rebecca Rayser
Daode	Richard Mason
Superintendent	Judyann Jonsson
Organising Secretary	Arthur French
Daoude	Robert Hooks
Segi	Rosalind Cash
	Frances Foster
Kongi	Moses Gunn

timations of Bertolt Brecht, "Kongi's Harvest" is straight political drama, told not only in narrative, but also in song and dance, masque, and choral ensembles, with penny-whistle flutes and tom-tom drums providing the musical accompaniment.

The skeletal structure on which the work is built is the conflict between an insurgent African tribal chieftain against the white-uniformed black Hitler who rules his country at the moment; the harvest of the title is the climactic moment at an annual ritual during which the tribal chieftain is called upon to present a symbolic yam to the dictator as a token of fealty the people bear their ruler.

A good deal of the language in which this business is couched may sound artificial and strange to unaccustomed ears ("Be not angry with us, O my king!" one of the tribal chieftain's women pleads with him. Or again, "You have split the gut of our make-believe!" exclaims another character at another point.) But from the moment the lights go up on the stage to reveal the populace massed together and thumbing their noses at the audience, and through such diversions as a hilarious meeting of an advisory council arguing ever a new image they must create for their nation ("Positive scientism," one of them suggests and to get rid of that troublesome chieftain would only be "a policy of glamorized fossilism") there are many passages in "Kongi's Harvest" demonstrating an exceptionally adroit and sharply satirical mind at work.

Two of the principal figures in the organization of the Negro Ensemble Company are also to be seen in two of the major roles of the drama. Douglas Turner Ward is a majestic and fiery figure as the insurgent tribal chief, and Robert Hooks is an eloquent and zealous heir to the throne. Moses Gunn, another stalwart from the same company, makes a terrifying black dictator, and Rosalind Cash is a subtle and menacing daughter of an executed rebel, seeking revenge for her father. Arthur French as an "organizing secretary," a henchman for the dictator; Afolabi Ajayi, a native Nigerian himself, as a captain of a "Carpenters Brigade," and Richard Mason as a young man who joins that brigade with no notion whatever of how to behave, are all notable in their separate assignments.

"Kongi's Harvest" is big, noisy and maybe a little pretentious in its effects. But there is no denying that it is also extraordinarily stimulating and provocative theater.

---

the village VOICE, April 18, 1968

THEATRE: KONGI'S HARVEST

A play by Wole Soyinka, presented by the Negro Ensemble Company at St. Mark's Playhouse through May 12. Directed by Michael A. Schultz

by A. D. Coleman

Currently imprisoned in Nigeria for "political activities," Wole Soyinka, while neither a revolutionary nor an agitator, is a writer concerned with his nation's problems, particularly those centering on its emergence into the 20th century. The subject of "Kongi's Harvest" is precisely that: set in the mythical nation of Isma on the eve of its national harvest celebration, the play explores the dilemmas involved in the inevitable development of any such nation and in the changing of the guard which occurs as modern forms of government replace traditional tribal leadership.

Kongi, the current ruler of Isma, is a half-fascist, half-communist dictator whose rule is threatened by dissension within his country. To establish harmony, Kongi demands that Oba Danlola (Douglas Turner), the most influential of the chieftains, symbolically deliver the First Yam—traditionally given to the gods in homage—to Kongi instead. Vast amounts of political intrigue surround this, however, and intricate plots must be woven to draw in the chief. Other complexities—the question of amnesty for five revolutionaries sentenced to death, the subversive intentions of Danlola's nephew and the heir to the throne (Robert Hooks), the machinations of Kongi's ex-mistress Segi (Rosalind Cash)—weave through the plot, thickening the texture and enriching the action.

Soyinka is a brilliant playwright, able to mix the masks of tribal ritual with the artificial personae of modern politics, the deep pulse of native drums with the reedy piping of national anthems. In all such opposites he looks for the common ground, sensing the relationships between them. His people are drawn with depth and intelligence, and he

stereotypes neither the younger Africans nor their elder. His sympathies lie with all his characters, a rare trait indeed.

The play's climax is a moment of stark Elizabethan horror, with echoes of the Salome legend. Soyinka has added an epilogue for comic relief, but it is unnecessary and actually irritating; the audience burst into prolonged applause at the climax as the lights dimmed, and the epilogue came as a disappointment.

The acting of Moses Gunn as Kongi, along with Douglas Turner, Robert Hooks and Rosalind Cash, stood out. Hooks, in particular, impresses me more each time I see him. The cast of approximately 40 is so large that singling out other performances would be hazardous; the ensemble was enthusiastic, well-rehearsed, and convincing in all save the first speech, which came out slightly garbled. Edward Burbridge has provided a deceptively simple four-level stage set, all stained wood; Jeanne Button's costumes are colorful, and she has improvised some highly effective masks. The direction is carefully paced; the entire production begins to percolate about halfway through the first act, and by the climax at the end of the second the theatre is pulsating feverishly. A very rewarding production.

Kongi's Harvest, Sole-Patrick Collaboration
From the Pat Patrick Archive

Pat Patrick was clearly aware of the connection between the struggles for independence among African nations and the struggle for civil rights in the United States. He was highly regarded and thought to be important to the success of these productions, to providing the musical settings and arrangements and to serving as the musical director. He was given charge to set the songs and direct the musicians. Pat Patrick knew the historical, political, creative culture at the time, and he valued what the music meant and how it would make an impact in these productions.

Reviews

The *Long Island Star Journal* in November 10, 1967, wrote "Soyinka Has a Sharp Pen."

> In his first two plays shown here, Wole Soyinka of Nigeria has a keen eye and a sharp pen. . . . The 33-year old writer has been under arrest in his homeland since August, accused of siding with the attempted succession of Nigeria from Biafra. Whatever his politics, the British-educated Soyinka admirably conveys a feeling that his plays accurately catch and mordantly comment on far-off nonpolitical circumstance.

New York Times, on November 10, 1967, under the headline "The Theater: 2 Plays by Nigerian Wole Soyinka," wrote "Belgrave is to be thanked for introducing us to a strong new voice in anybody's theater. Now let us hope for some good news from Nigeria."

Wall Street Journal on this same day wrote, "An African View of Africa": "The small stage of the Greenwich Theater is exploding these nights with the stunning bright colors of Nigerian fabrics and imagery. And more importantly, the first professional production in the U.S. of the plays of Wole Soyinka, heralded as Africa's leading playwright, is an impressive and welcomed occasion."

Daily News, on November 10, 1967, had another positive review. In "Show Business: Nigerian Double Bill Interesting Stage Fare," the reviewer wrote, "It will be no small consolation to Soyinka that we found it an unusual and interesting evening in the theater, but to the producers and the players, it might serve as a kind of morale booster during the enforced absence of the playwright."

New York Post, on November 10, 1967, reported "Two on the Isle, Play by an African Dramatist." The reviewer noted, "This justifies all the enthusiastic things I heard about him in his native Nigeria two summers ago."

Time magazine, on November 17, 1967, wrote "Infectious Humanity," stating, "He [Soyinka] is emancipated without being alienated. Blending mock humor with flare-lit passion. He is both satirist and myth poet."

New York Amsterdam News, on November 18, 1967, in "2 Fine Plays by Nigerian Soyinka," wrote, "As the play progresses one begins to see that the good-hearted and unsuspecting Scott is destined to meet a tragic end. . . . Soyinka was able to convince the audience that disaster was eminent. . . . Soyinka has masterfully put together a series of scenes which keep everyone in the audience constantly guessing and trying to figure out what will happen next."

New Yorker, on November, 18, 1967, in its off-Broadway Theater section wrote, "*The Strong Breed* is tragic but is not depressing and surely part of the excitement one feels when watching it comes from the recognition of its complete authenticity."

West Side New Free Press, on November 23, 1967, stated, "The sight and sounds of Soyinka's play are fresh . . . [and] offer an indication of his talents, and offer us an image of society where the Black is not such a slave to man as to an idea of the past."

Villager, on November 23, 1967, wrote that the play "holds one's interest because of the fearful judgment that is to be carried out."

"African Music in the Space Age," as *New York Free Press* called it, wonderfully moves beyond the global connections here to see Pat Patrick making connections through his "musical father," Sun Ra.

In the *Morning Telegraph*, on April 15, 1968, the reviewer noted, "the verdict today can be nothing else than that Mr. Soyinka may again attract a good deal of favorable attention. This new presentation is a much more ambitious effort than the two simple little one-acters."

Daily News, on April 16, 1968, reported "Nigerian Play Rousing Tale of Power Struggle," stating, "The Negro ensemble is perhaps the most exuberant group of players ever to take to the stage. They like a stage piece they can get their teeth into and shake all over the place. They have such a property in their newest production, *Kongi's Harvest*, a melodramatic political work by Wole Soyinka."

In *New York Free Press* on April 25, 1968, in the review entitled "Theater: A Snapshot for a History Still to Be Developed," the reviewer noted,

> *Kongi*, like Africa itself, offers a spectacle of change, a mixture which will seem to American audiences both familiar and strange. The play can really be criticized only out of its own tradition. It is a tableau, not a melodrama. The satire which sometimes seems hackneyed or merely facile is nonetheless bold within its tradition. . . . His play is a snapshot for a history still to be developed. It captures African life at a pivotal silence, when both ruler and ruled know each other's boundaries and the continent waits, in Franz Fanon's words, for its people to discover a mission, and fulfill it or betray it.

One understands that these reviews focused on more than the entertainment value and artistry of the plays. The focus was also on the politics. The Wole Soyinka plays in this productive period made an impact on New York audiences, and Pat Patrick and his music were essential to this success.

In conversations we had about this with Mr. Soyinka, he stated his regret that he did not have the chance to know Pat Patrick better. As he put it,

> Sad thing is, however, that I did not know Pat Patrick and only vaguely recall a meeting with a musician at a New York tea party with Amiri Baraka. We never did spend time together. I cannot even offer any informed commentary on his music. I had nothing to do with the productions. I did meet the director and lead actor of *Kongi's Harvest* some time later but never did see a performance. I took in shows by the ensemble, but not one of mine. I believe I was sojourning in prison when *Kongi's Harvest* was presented.
>
> One, two, three, four years after I came out of prison, my friend, a filmmaker who had been marginally involved in those "in absentia" productions—simply as an interested friend, unofficially consulted, especially during the *Brother Jero/Strong Breed* bill.
>
> I have no knowledge of Pat Patrick's connection, no idea about the music, the direction, interpretation, or other artistic aspects. It is possible, quite possible, that I saw snatches of these reviews after I came out of prison. The paired one-act debut was initiated by a young Nigerian, then resident in New York. He has since died and his name keeps eluding me. After that experience, he relocated to Nigeria and we met. He surely brought with him a dossier of photos and clippings to show me, but my mind retained none of this. In effect, I'm seeing the reviews for the first time.

Though Soyinka may not have realized it at the time, his trial in Nigeria was clearly a global expression that resonated in the States, particularly among American Blacks during this time who saw him as revolutionary. During these days of independence, African people were pursuing liberation from colonial and even Black African powers. This pursuit inspired African American audiences, as can be seen by the excitement around the Soyinka productions.

Soyinka could be seen as a writer, voice, a champion of truth. Black nationalism was being read from outside as a sign of Black global solidarity. It was during this time that Bob Marley's eyes, in a very few years forward, would be fixed on Curtis Mayfield and others whose music "was the call" of the era. But were the works handled in a way that potentially got the messages through? Did the narrative voice of wisdom and experience still connect deeply in ways that served the intended meaning?

In 1968, *Kongi's Harvest* was produced as a more serious work. Soyinka, in this critical New York theater arena, is met with "the verdict today can be nothing else than that Mr. Soyinka may again attract a good deal of favorable attention. This new presentation is a much more ambitious effort than the two simple little one-acters."

Beyond what might be a lot of extra exposure due to the world's interest in Africa's plight and flight from a century of colonial holds, the highly visible, culturally political and sensitive Soyinka court case and Soyinka as one of the era's "most celebrated political prisoners," there is a fair amount of genuine excitement and critical appreciation of his work as good theater with meaningful punch and patter.

From all accounts, it's compelling that as a creative thinker Soyinka's work was fruiting. This was a time when the world needed to hear and be moved, and Black artists in particular were focused on "truth pressed to the earth having to rise." Yet the truth here was that this was all going on without Soyinka fully knowing the impact the work was having. Until this publication, he had never seen any of these reviews in context, and, at the time, he was unaware that audiences were being moved by the ideas in his works in print. These reviews from local newspapers were all collected, cut, and pasted onto the backs of cardboard poster announcements of the productions, each one by Pat Patrick himself, preserved all these years in his private and fully archived collection. These treasures were left to his children.

Again, on Soyinka's part, the ideas had landed, been cemented, and were delivered widely and deeply received. Although there are many successes to speak of, getting music and theater works staged and people in the seats, getting the clear success of recognition and documentation of creative work, and having legitimately, critically acclaimed projects consistently in the worlds' largest theater town is a huge musical accomplishment.

This is within the first six or seven years of Pat Patrick's creative time in New York, and the 1970s and the 1980s are still ahead.

Friends of Pat Patrick, 1960s and 1970s
From the Pat Patrick Archive

Friends of Pat Patrick, 1960s and 1970s
From the Pat Patrick Archive

RECORD WORLD'S ALL STAR BAND/NEW ARTIST

What follows is a letter Patrick received awarding him the honor of *Record World*'s "All Star Band/New Artist" in 1968.

200 west 57th street, new york, new york 10019

Circle 7-6250

April 25, 1968

Mr. Pat Patrick
513 Fifth Street
Apt. 2C
New York, New York 10003

Dear Mr. Patrick:

For the first time in the history of the trade, an important publication has devoted a special issue to the Jazz musician and Jazz records. As the Jazz Editor of Record World Magazine, and as a Jazz broadcaster, I am extremely proud of this special Jazz issue published by Record World Magazine April 27, 1968.

We are also particularly proud that you have been selected as "Record World All-Star Band/New Artist".

Sometime during the latter part of May or the first week in June, it will be our pleasure to invite you to a cocktail party at which time the presentation of your award will be made. Since many of the outstanding performers from the world of Jazz will be invited to attend, I sincerely hope that you will be able to arrange your schedule to enable you to be present.

Sincerely,

Del Shields
Jazz Editor

DS:ivd

P.S. A copy of our special Jazz Issue is enclosed for your pleasure.

Letter from Del Shields, 1968
From the Pat Patrick Archive

· 6 ·

Artistry, New York 1970–1979

Hook this in with the beat article. . . . This column is open for
suggestions, inquiries and any letters dealing with Black music
from a folklore, historical or contemporary points of view. With
the idea in mind that this should become a healthy avenue for
exchange of ideas and information. . . . To find out how to
cripple and destroy the system, find out where it gets its fuel
and power, just as fire must have oxygen to burn. . . . Do a play
on "the philosophy in Black Blues singers." Prepare for your
seed sown.

—From Pat Patrick archive notes

THE 1970s

The decade of the 1970s opened up for Pat Patrick in a symbolic way; it was
as if he had "arrived." Charlie Rouse, a stable member of the much-admired
Thelonious Monk group, left the band, and a Chicago friend of Pat's, Wilbur
Ware, recommended Pat to Thelonious. Pat brushed up on his tenor work
and ended up working with this leading jazz thinker for six months, playing
at major jazz venues, including Village Vanguard in New York, and touring
in Boston and Philadelphia.

In 1972 came the creation of the Baritone Retinue Ensemble. Pat formed
this group with his old Chicago buddy Charles Davis. Pat and the group were
highlighted on Amiri Baraka's well-followed New Jersey TV show, and with
Amiri's advice, they recorded the disc *Sound Advice*. Pat's many connections
and his own focus as an enterprising, gigging first-call musician brought him

59

to play in orchestras on Broadway and in traveling shows, including *The Wiz,* *Bubbling Brown Sugar,* and Bob Fosse's *Dancin'*.

The discussion among musicians interested in "nation time" and Black consciousness and culture aroused another deep passion in Pat in terms of educating the youth. As many learned jazz musicians began to be called upon to teach in college programs, Pat Patrick began teaching at the State University of New York, Old Westbury College. Following Sun Ra's interesting appointment teaching classes in Black history, Pat also taught traditional arranging and composition.

Looking at the list of musical activities ahead during the 1970s, one can argue that Pat Patrick's fruitful and varied work as an active musician in New York continued. Things were happening in many directions now. Regular, steady gigging for a working musician in New York is huge. It is from this that many professional contacts arise. A musician establishes his working business relationships, and the ones already in place are sweetened. A musician gets a "rep" and that get him calls. Pat's reputation for reliability and his fame in the jazz industry blossomed. In addition to everything else, he was appointed as musical editor for the *Black Theatre Magazine*.

Pat Patrick writes from his resume,

- Wrote and played music for a dance production that was to be put on Broadway called *Jessica* by Melvin Van Peebles, who has a movie that he directed due for release starring Godfry Cambridge
- More college campuses on the West coast with Sun Ra, also Newport Jazz Festival and Boston Globe Festival, 1969
- Did summer teaching in the lower Manhattan community for the city of New York Parks and Recreation and Cultural Affairs
- Played and recorded for a film made by modern organization of Dance Involvement Inc., division of State Council on the Arts
- Played briefly with Cesar Conception Orchestra from Puerto Rico and with Joe Quijano
- More recently played with Thelonious Monk

ARRIVALS

Pat Patrick, by the 1970s, had come fully into the New York jazz community in a way that can only be spoken of as the proper arrival. When musicians dream about being in the right place at the right time, doing what they want to do with the right groups of people, that is "arriving."

Cuban composer Denis Peralto commented, "The opportunity to live about your art, your creations, your performances, and your ideas, or dreams coming through is immense! That's the goal in life, when you can make your realities your dreams is the highest level of living."[1]

After a decade full of performing as a sideman, recording and directing ensembles for theater pieces, and touring, Pat Patrick opened this decade performing with one of the most celebrated artists in modern jazz, Thelonious Monk.

As Robin Kelley writes in *Thelonious Monk: The Life and Times of An American Original*,

> Monk scrambled to find a saxophonist to finish out the week at the Vanguard. Ed Blackwell suggested Dewey Redman . . . but Redman turned down the offer. . . . Wilbur Ware then suggested baritone saxophonist "Laurdine Pat Patrick," a fellow Chicagoan trained by the legendary Captain Walter Dyett, at Dusable High School. He grew up in a musician family, having studied piano, drums, and trumpet before switching to alto then baritone saxophone. Patrick was best known for his work with Sun Ra and Mongo Santamaria, although he had worked quite a bit with traveling artists who played Chicago's Regal Theatre—notably Nat "King" Cole, Don Redman, Illinois Jacquet, Cootie Williams, and a parade of singers. Patrick had played across many genres, from swing to Latin to avant-garde, and he was an excellent improviser.[2]

Sun Ra at Theatre des Amandiers
From the Pat Patrick Archive

Mar. 7, 1970   **THE**   Price 50 cents

NEW YORKER

February 19th, Thelonious Monk started a three-day stint with a new quartet at the Village Vanguard, which for thirty years has been one of the best places in the world to hear jazz. Monk carries his own universe within him, and this evening it was apparently in whirling sync, for he was brilliant. He was wearing a new tall black fur hat, recently given him in Toronto, but he didn't dance, cavort, or fidget; he simply played, and with a freshness and intensity he hasn't always shown in the past few years. Monk's new group – the old one revolved for eight years around the tenor saxophonist Charlie Rouse—includes Pat Patrick on tenor saxophone, Wilbur Ware on bass, and Beaver Harris on drums.

Ware was a member of the stunning group Monk had for a while in 1957 (John Coltrane and Shadow Wilson were also in it), and he probably has a good deal to do with Monk's rejuvenation.

Patrick, who plays somewhat in the manner of Lucky Thompson, seems awed by Monk.

It was a consummate evening.

—Whitney Balliett

1970 Performance with Thelonious Monk
From the Pat Patrick Archive

John Gilmore in New York
From the Pat Patrick Archive

Sun Ra Musicians in New York 1960s
From the Pat Patrick Archive

Sun Ra, August 1964
From the Pat Patrick Archive

Arkestra Member
From the Pat Patrick Archive

Sun Ra in Motion
From the Pat Patrick Archive

THE LEFT BANK JAZZ SOCIETY

PROUDLY PRESENTS FOR 1976

SUN RA

and his Myth Science
Cosmos Swing Arkestra

"An evening with SUN RA and his Cosmic Swing Arkestra is an evening of mystery, joy, pageantry and a trip through space, time, dreams and layers of music that add up to an experience unlike any other; part sanctified church, part boody-bump-beautiful business, part mystic giggles and satire, part swing to the max!"

Stanley Crouch [Noted Jazz writer]
September 1976 - New York City

SUNDAY, OCTOBER 10, 1976 — 5 p. m.

"What he offered was both more than music and more than musical theater...Sixteen men dressed in outrageously cut-rate space garb, carried on for hours without pause. The music spanned all of jazz history."

Bob Blumenthal
Boston Globe - 1976

Famous Ballroom
1717 N. Charles Street   Baltimore, Md.

For Further Information Call   A NON-PROFIT   For Subscribing Membership Write
JAZZ LINE 945-2266   ORGANIZATION   L.B.J.S. 2559 Frederick Avenue

Sun Ra at Left Bank Jazz Society
From the Pat Patrick Archive

Patrick echoed the sentiments of virtually every musician who had worked with Monk when he said: "How educational it was for me to be associated with him during that period."

The 1970s for Pat was a time too of full-bodied performances and musical activities as a player with his mentor, Sun Ra. The Sun Ra Arkestra was in full form and began the decade with what was called the "Grand Tour of Europe." The photographs from the Pat Patrick archives show an energized, youthful, and excited ensemble, twenty artists, musicians, singers, and dancers with Ra. This group is made up now of at least two sets of generations with Sun Ra part of the "original crew"—including members Pat Patrick, Marshall Allen, John Gilmore, and James Jackson—and what author John F. Szwed describes as a "younger, more aggressive post–civil rights generation."[3] This matters because as we are examining Pat Patrick's career, one is reminded that he starts out with Sun Ra, recruited in 1949 at the age of twenty. In 1970, he was now forty-one years old, the senior member influencing a new generation.

The first performance, at the Fondation Maeght in Saint Paul de Vence, France, was an accepted venue for the European avant-garde and had hosted everyone from Picasso to American composer John Cage. Sun Ra's music was, in some cases, shocking. Most people in the audience had never seen a Black avant-garde orchestra. Sun Ra—with many wind players, percussionists, dancers, and singers in space costumes and with his use of a synthesizer—was a theater spectacle who wowed Europe. With concerts in 1970 and 1971, the orchestra returned twice to Europe during this period. As one critic noted, "His UK first performance was one of the most spectacular concerts ever held in this country. Moog synthesizer, futuristic lyrics . . . sung by June Tyson . . . saxophone riffs repeated over and over by Pat Patrick and Danny Thompson . . . while John Gilmore shredded and blistered a ribbon of multiphonics from his tenor." Here we find Patrick referred to as a prominent and significant performer as part of the well-established Sun Ra Arkestra, now an international phenomenon. These performances made enough noise to make an impression. At one performance at the Kongresshalle, West Berlin, November 7, 1971, as author Szwed explains, "The dramatic power of Ra's work and members is evident as Ra called out 'Pat Patrick' to summon up what New York musicians called 'energy music.'"[4]

BACK HOME

In the spring of 1971, Sun Ra was appointed lecturer at the University of California, Berkeley, in the department of Afro-American studies. The course, "The Black Man in the Cosmos," had a reading list that included the young radical poet Leroi Jones, also known as Amiri Baraka.

Within a year, Pat Patrick would become appointed to teach, too, becoming an adjunct professor at the State University of New York, Old Westbury College. There was by now a wave of such appointments of jazz performers in the college classroom, who were now respected as professionals who would bring their expertise and knowledge of "the Black experience" to the classroom, as Black studies and jazz were being integrated into college curricula.

All across the country, colleges and universities were beginning Black studies programs. Soon Archie Shepp, Dr. Billy Taylor, James Baldwin, Fred Tillis, and Max Roach would all be teaching and/or heading up Afro-American and jazz studies programs. The program at the University of Massachusetts, Amherst, is one prominent example. Sun Ra was trained as an education major when he was a college student. Teaching was a natural next step for him. Again, he seemed to be always prepared for the future and his protégé Patrick was also well positioned.

These were the larger cultural forces at work as Baraka, Sun Ra, Pat Patrick, and others who felt "called upon" were able to extend the experience and culture of the "Black man" into the educational curriculum.

1972

1972 was a big year for Patrick. He recorded the album *Space Is the Place* with the Sun Ra Arkestra on ABC/Impulse records. He also won a talent poll established at *Downbeat Magazine*. And he founded, with Charles Davis, the Baritone Saxophone Retinue Band. The brochure described the band this way:

An introduction to the Baritone Saxophone Retinue. Years ago, the so-called jazz bands very frequently used two baritones and a bass saxophone or two along with the many woodwind instruments that were played by the members of their reed sections. Of all the saxophones used in these bands, it is our opinion that the one with the most distinctive sound, warmth, and range that can reach into that of the other saxophones, is the baritone sax. Yet it has less exposure and popularity than the others.

However, it is the barry sax that ties the others together in the making of a really fine reed section of a band, as witnessed in the Duke Ellington Orchestra.

We cite the Duke's orchestra because it has been through the innovation of his writing for the reeds, that an institution of reed section playing has developed and is widely used in bands of today.

THE ARRIVAL OF NEW MUSICAL IMPULSES

One of the interesting things about Pat Patrick, as with many working musicians at this time, is his reaction to the arrival of mainstream popular music forces. The early driving question to the Patrick inquiry we raised was: what were the forces Pat was reacting to? By 1965, Pat Patrick had created a popular song, "Yeh Yeh," which had become a hit in Great Britain. This song was both a symbol of his success and a symbol of white pop singers acculturating Black sounds. Let us explain.

English artist Georgie Fame and the Blue Flames recorded this song to huge success. This is a twist in the tale that was to provide an interesting note in the jazz trajectory of Patrick's work, particularly in the late 1970s and into the 1980s. "Yeh Yeh" was cowritten by pianist Rodgers Grant and Pat Patrick and first recorded in 1963 by Mongo Santamaria. Pat was then a band member of Mongo's band along with Grant. From the Andrew Hill, Down Pat recording, the buoyant sax line that drives it with a kind of boogie-woogie blues arpeggiated figure became a staple lick among many emerging R&B and early rock-and-roll pieces, and "Yeh Yeh" was no different. So appealing was this Patrick-Grant tune that it was also recorded by Gerald Wilson, Baby Cortez, and Jerry Fielding and the Hollywood Brass, and it later was used in the 1987 movie *Good Morning Vietnam*. On that soundtrack, the song was listed as "Yeh Yeh," written by Pat Patrick, Rodgers Grant, performed by Georgie Flame and the Blue Flames, courtesy of Polygram Records.

"Yeh Yeh" came to the attention of the great jazz singer Jon Hendricks, who added lyrics and recorded it on a *Jazz at Newport '63 Live* album. English pop singer Georgie Fame then heard the Newport recording and was moved enough to incorporate it into his live Blue Flames shows.

The song was so catchy that someone in Georgie Fame's camp persuaded him to record it as a single. Fame's attempts to have "Yeh Yeh" played on the BBC and Radio Luxembourg were blocked because, as one report stated, the station complained it sounded "too Black." Unable to get airplay, Georgie Fame became part of group that set up the ship-based pirate radio station Radio Caroline in March 1964.

This station played the song and gave it heavy rotation. It worked. Without help from the conventional radio stations, "Yeh Yeh" topped the UK charts in January 1965 (US #25), knocking the Beatles off their five-week top spot.

All this was a part of the interesting wave of British pop that came to be known as the British invasion. It's interesting that this song, along with many other British covers of American R&B or soul tunes, gave rise to the familiarity of these artists. But, ironically, they were replacing the original American and certainly the Black musicians who originated the music.

We find traces of Pat Patrick's feelings and ideas about popular music some ten years after this, when he wrote,

> The original sounds that have had so much to do with the foundation of our culture have through the ages been used and misused for all sorts of purposes other than what the music was intended for. Seems that the music often heard these days no matter how one thinks he enjoys it, is not contributing enough toward the greater awareness of Black folks. . . . Many benefits derived from his [the Black man's] work has been diverted from him and his people by something or other. This is no accident but rather a carefully worked-out conspiracy.

By the time "Our Music: Yesterdays, Todays and Tomorrows," Patrick's essay reflecting these concerns, had been written, there had been major cultural shifts, and popular music had at least two effects on jazz musicians of this earlier generation: (1) Patrick's concern about the decline in "quality" music, a major tenet that defined his work, and (2) the reduction in the number of "calls" he received.

By the 1980s, the work, calls, and gigs had slowed proportionally to the rise of other forms of popular music, namely rock, soul, and what Patrick called "jive music," or the lesser forms of music. Other cities, including Chicago (with Chess records) and Detroit (with Motown), produced an explosion of popular music, artists, and culture, and that began to grow and affect the soil of popular tastes in an increasingly competitive popular music marketplace. These styles would compete with jazz throughout the 1960s and 1970s. Technology also competed with live musicians. By the 1980s, many musicians were simply replaced by drum machines, programmers, and clap tracks.

But these changes had been brewing slowly for decades. Atlantic Records in the 1940s with R&B artists like Lavern Baker, Ruth Brown, and Solomon Burke and then Sun Records in Memphis as early as 1952 introduced pieces of a "new sound," the early rockabilly, rock-and-roll records that began to bring together both Black and white teens, broadening the base of popular music.

Sun Ra's soundtrack for the 1957 film *Cry of Jazz* underlined the principal argument that jazz was the only music that could address the role of the Black man in America. Sun Ra formulated a future aesthetic. But the popular music market was formulating its own answers, and it was a music for teens now. The dominance of jazz began to see its end. By the time the 1960s impulses emerged with the Brill building pop writers, New York, Phil

Spector, and then the Beatles' arrival in 1964, followed by the larger British invasion, there was also Motown's "Sound of Young America" and "Dancing in the Streets." Things were set then to shift drastically. The marketplace was crowded now with new trends, styles, and faces, and jazz musicians would begin to have more competition than they did in the early 1960s. Once the market had ramped itself up to this new rock-and-roll and there was a new buying public with new technologies including the transistor radio, this all had a devastating effect on the old guard of traditional jazz players.

Few survived it. Sun Ra did, but he suffered. As we saw earlier, he had made plans for the future. But he had to contend with this and diversify his playing or be destroyed by the competition. Clubs that once drew audiences closed or transformed in order to meet the demands of youth drawn to popular fads, dances, and styles.

Pat Patrick had to make some adjustments.

The constant rise of popular music, the current movement of the avant-garde aesthetic, the 1970s sociopolitical turbulence, and Patrick's social and personal family realities all made it difficult for him. The jazz musician was beginning to have less of an impact on the identity and interests of the post-1960s youth.

Pat Patrick weathered this and was still riding well through his workings, but it is in his writing that we see these cultural shifts and concerns clearly. Archie Schepp, Charles Mingus, John Coltrane, and others were to emerge as a more radical strain of jazz, which took center stage for a millisecond in a movement called "the New Thing." But the new faces of popular culture were a force jazz musicians had to deal with, and Pat Patrick was no different, despite his stellar recording and performing record. Things and times had changed; the culture had shifted. And his children had grown in all these years.

SON DEVAL PATRICK COMES TO NEW YORK

In 1974, the summer before Pat's son Deval Patrick began at Harvard, Deval was admitted into a management training internship program in New York on Wall Street. Deval arrived in New York needing a place to stay and decided to live with his father for a short period. There had been some contact over the years with the children. At the time, Pat was living in Queens. During that summer, some bad feelings and misunderstandings ultimately brewed.

As Deval shared, "Our lifestyle, Wall Street work, was the final surrender to capitalism, in his view, to the white power structure, to the institutions that had oppressed Blacks forever. This was what Milton, Harvard, and my mother had begot."

Given the times and Pat's issues with "the man's system," this feeling of resentment flowered in many ways. Pat Patrick's disapproval of his son at this time was heightened by the social rage and tensions of the times. But that, too, would change and Pat would mellow. As Deval Patrick writes of his father's countercultural lifestyle:

> Pat was big on health food and herbal tea long before it came into fashion. . . . My father had a special charm, especially with women. . . . An intense man with great powers of concentration, he was his most engaged, his most emotionally present, when riffing a jazz set. . . . He was also passionate about football. He knew the players, the teams, the standings, the history.[5]

The civil rights pushes of the 1960s and 1970s should have offered hope to Blacks, but in some ways that hopeful sentiment hardened to rage as the reality set in that things were not changing for good or fast enough. The relationship between Pat and Deval, as told by Deval, was more of a prodigal father who had fled than the other way around. And yet one can see the maturation of both father and son as they develop a caring relationship through the 1980s, until Pat's eventual death in 1991.

In 1978 and 1979, after graduating from Harvard, Deval traveled to Sudan, the motherland of Africa. His mother Emily met him there, another touching crossroads in the Patrick family story. These were the years Deval made both the connection to Africa and gained his father's admiration in new ways.

Despite the son's academic and growing professional successes, it was his visit to Sudan and his familiarity through study and living within cotemporary African culture that helped to change the dynamics between the father and son.

Due to his son's visit to the mother continent, Pat, who was a conscious Black nationalist artist, stopped thinking that Deval was not "Black enough." Africa, African dashikis, Afros, and soul was "Black power" to him. A visit to the motherland gave Deval credibility and helped Pat to stop judging him. Interestingly, as well, Deval Patrick grew closer to his mother, Emily, at this time. She had moved to New York, and the Patrick family was reunited, at least geographically, albeit through aging, the marriages of the children, and the births of grandchildren. The 1980s were a new era that cemented the directions of a son, now married with children, and raised questions about the stability and industry support for the aging musician father.

FROM PAT PATRICK'S RESUME, LETTERS, AND MORE

Resume

• Recorded with Clifford Thorton and the Jazz Composers Orchestra, April 4, 1974, New York
• Recorded with Grachan Moncur, Jazz Composers Orchestra Association, April 11, 1974
• Composite list of participating players (Pat Patrick, Hannibal Marvin Peterson, Wadda Leo Smith, Dewy Redman, Carla Bley, Leroy Jenkins, Cecil Mcbee, Charlie Haden, Beaver Harris)
• Recorded with Robert Northern, Brother Asah, March, 9, 1975, New York, Divine Recordings
• Recorded with Rahsaan Roland Kirk, the Case of the 3-Sided Dream in Audio Color, May 14, 1975, Atlantic Recordings
• Sam Wooding, Bicentennial Jazz Vistas, 1976, New York, Twin Sign Recording
• Famous Ballroom, Baltimore Maryland, with Sun Ra
• Recording, Live at Montreux: Sun Ra and His Arkestra, July 9, 1976, Pat Patrick, Rhonda Patrick, dancer
• Recorded with Clifford Jordan and his band Inward Fire, April 5, 1977, Muse Recordings
• Recorded with Bobby Watson, June 29, 30, August 1, October 27, 28, 1977, New York
• 1978–1979 Henry Street Settlement, New Federal Theater, with Amiri Baraka
• Awarded Music Excellence Award, June 23, 1979, Consortium of Jazz Organizations
• Playing in D.C. with Band
• Stanley Cowell, New World, November 1978, Berkeley, Galaxy Recordings

Letters

3/18/1977

Hey Ed Smith.
    Hope this little note finds you doing fine and taking care of business. My main man Ronnie Boykins who was snowbound with you awhile ago when he was working with Mary Lou Williams told me you had checked them out and gave him the word that you had asked about me.

So I'd thought I'd contact you to let you know what I'm into these days. I've been with S.U.N.Y. for about a year and a half now and it's been nice. Also good experience for me, to which I'm enclosing some information on that. Also my group is doing a little gig soon (the 28th of March) that I'd thought I'd hip you to just in case you might be in town that day.

And last, I'm including some info on the group just in case a concert or seminar might turn up in your area that you might feel that we could take part in.

Don't hesitate to drop me a line any way either at my N.Y. box number or here at the college. I'd like to hear from you. Perhaps we can do something on the scholastic level too.

Take care, straight ahead.
Pat Patrick

7/26/1979 (Letter from Pat to Amiri Baraka)

Hey AB
I forget to mention on the phone today, that Ed Bland called to ask if I had heard if Sonny was back and that he thought you had gone with the band this time. Here's the run down for the label:

Sound Advice: The Baritone Saxophone Retinue
Side 1
Stalemates (B. Golsen)
Funny time (J. Heath)
Uptightedness (P. Patrick)
Eastern Vibrations (C. Davis)
Side 2
Sabia (A. Jobim)
East of UZ (Sun Ra)
The Waltz (C. Davis)
Stablemates (B. Golsen)

I don't have the broadcast societies for all the tunes, but I don't think it is necessary on the label. I'll do some research and get it together for the jacket cover. Also let me know if it would be an inconvenience or appropriate to release the same LP on another label if somebody makes me an offer that could be beneficial, like a sublease or what have you. That's all I can think of for now except a beige or red color for the label paper would be nice. Something that will stand out. Look to hear from you soon.

Pat

PS. The LP will be called "Sound Advice" by the Baritone Saxophone Retinue

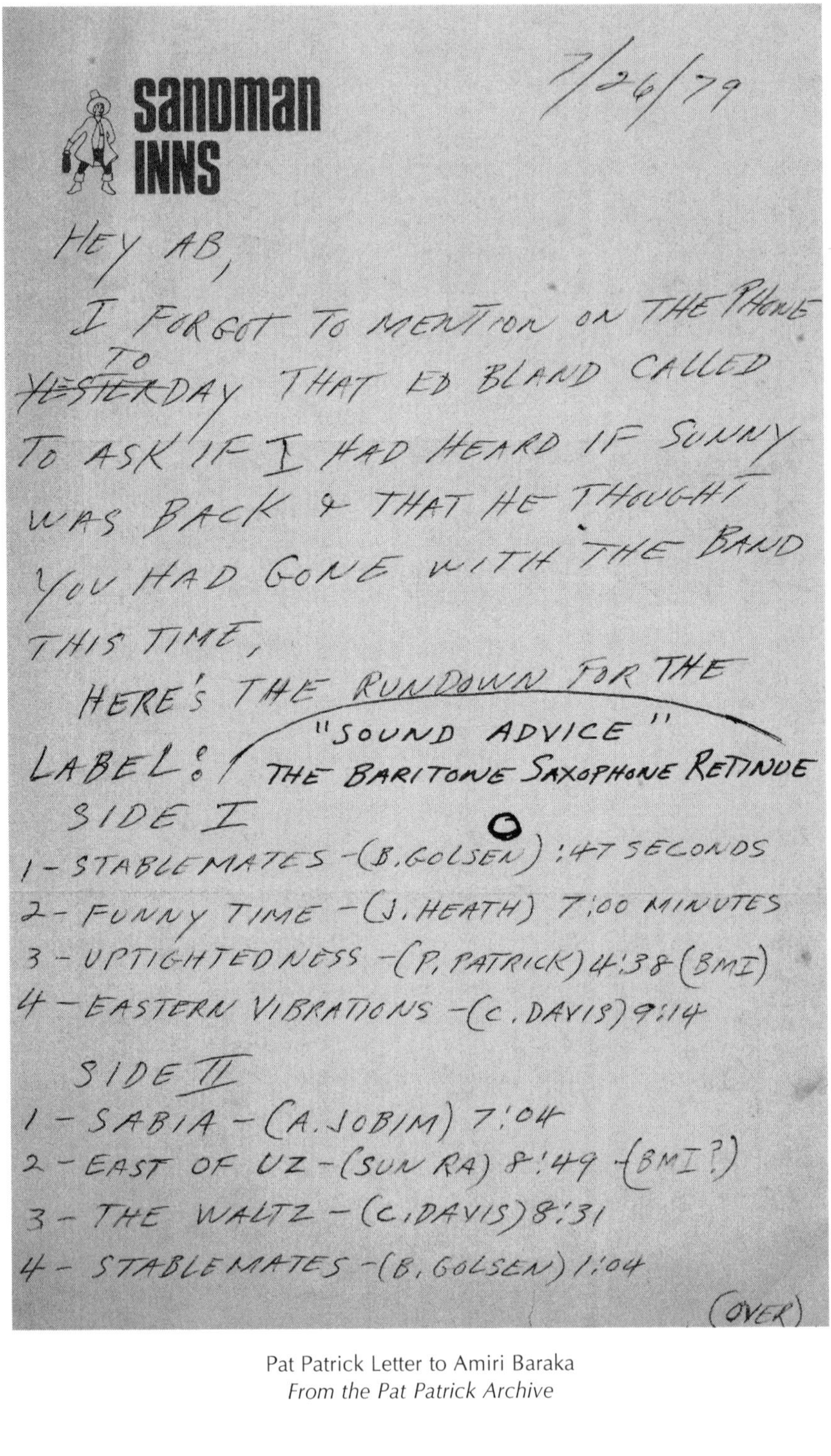

sandman INNS

7/26/79

HEY AB,

I FORGOT TO MENTION ON THE PHONE ~~YESTERDAY~~ TO THAT ED BLAND CALLED TO ASK IF I HAD HEARD IF SUNNY WAS BACK & THAT HE THOUGHT YOU HAD GONE WITH THE BAND THIS TIME.

HERE'S THE RUNDOWN FOR THE LABEL: / "SOUND ADVICE" / THE BARITONE SAXOPHONE RETINUE

SIDE I

1 — STABLE MATES — (B. GOLSEN) :47 SECONDS
2 — FUNNY TIME — (J. HEATH) 7:00 MINUTES
3 — UPTIGHTEDNESS — (P. PATRICK) 4:38 (BMI)
4 — EASTERN VIBRATIONS — (C. DAVIS) 9:14

SIDE II

1 — SABIA — (A. JOBIM) 7:04
2 — EAST OF UZ — (SUN RA) 8:49 (BMI?)
3 — THE WALTZ — (C. DAVIS) 8:31
4 — STABLE MATES — (B. GOLSEN) 1:04

(OVER)

Pat Patrick Letter to Amiri Baraka
From the Pat Patrick Archive

I DON'T HAVE THE BROADCAST SOCIETIES FOR ALL THE TUNES BUT I DON'T THINK IT IS NESSASARY ON THE LABEL, I'LL DO SOME RESERCH AND GET IT TOGETHER FOR THE JACKET COVER.

ALSO LET ME KNOW IF IT WOULD BE AN INCONVIENCE OR INAPPROPRIATE TO RELEASE THE SAME LP ON ANOTHER LABEL IF SOMEBODY MAKES ME AN OFFER THAT COULD BE BENEFICIAL, LIKE A SUB-LEASE OR WHAT HAVE YOU,

THAT'S ALL I CAN THINK OF FOR NOW EXCEPT A BIEGE OR RED COLOR FOR THE LABEL PAPER WOULD BE NICE, SOMETHING THAT WILL STAND OUT,

LOOK TO HEAR FROM YOU SOON,

Pat

P.S.
THE LP WILL BE CALLED
"SOUND ADVICE" BY THE BARITONE SAXOPHONE RETINUE

Pat Patrick letter to Amiri Baraka
From the Pat Patrick Archive

CHARLES DAVIS AND THE BARITONE SAXOPHONE RETINUE

FEATURING CECIL PAYNE
PAT PATRICK • KENNY ROGERS
KENNETH SINGLETARY
JACK WILSON ON PIANO
LARRY RIDLEY ON BASS
EDDIE GLADDEN ON DRUMS
AUGUST 5-6, 1983 • 10 PM-2 AM
JAZZ CULTURAL THEATRE
368 8 AVE., NYC. NEAR 28 ST.
DONATION $6 • (212) 244-0997
SPONSORED BY THE NATIONAL ENDOWMENT FOR THE ARTS

⊕ THE REVIEW OF AUG 7-/83
IS ON THIS GIG (A SAX QUINTET)

Charles Davis with Retinue
From the Pat Patrick Archive

Baritone Retinue in Performance
From the Pat Patrick Archive

Baritone Retinue Brochure, 1977
From the Pat Patrick Archive

Baritone Retinue Brochure, 1977
From the Pat Patrick Archive

Liner Notes

"SOUND ADVICE"
Produced by Pat Patrick, Alton Abraham, 1977, El Saturn records, Chicago, Illinois, the Baritone Saxophone Retinue

Personnel:

Pat Patrick
Charles Davis
Mario Rivera
Kenny Rogers
James Ware
Rene McLean
George Barrow
Reynold Scott

Rhythm section:

Hilton Ruiz, piano
Steve Solder, drums
Jon Hart, bass
Babafemi Humphreys, conga

Selections: Stablemates, Funny Times, Uprightedness (Patrick), Eastern Vibrations (Davis), Sambia, East of Uz (Sun Ra), The Waltz (Davis), Stablemates

"Sound Advice" for new horizons and potentials from a less-popular member of the saxophone family, the baritone. To illustrate that an instrument with such a range of possibilities can do more than just function at the bottom of reed sections is what this first release by the Baritone Saxophone Retinue is about. The use of more than one baritone in reed sections is not, however, a new concept, as can be seen when viewing photos of some of the early bands during the pre-swing era. There would be at times so many wooded instruments lined up in front of the reed section (along with other instruments they would double on) that it would almost obscure the musicians.

Although Charles Davis and I spent time together in the Sun Ra Arkestra in its early Chicago years, one was more likely to play among groups of similar instruments in a marching or concert band–type setting.

The idea for an all-baritone sax group was eventually put together in 1972 and represents what we feel is a first of its kind.

I will always cherish Harry Carney's reaction to hearing tapes of the group, as well as that of my former woodwind teacher during high school days, Willie Randall.

We therefore dedicate these sounds to the great pioneers (in the idiom) of the baritone saxophone: Harry Carney, Jack Washington, Eddie Barefield, Leslie Jonakins, Leo Parker, and Charlie Fawlkes, to name just a few. It is a little-known fact that some of these artists actually aided the various manufacturers in developing certain aspects of the mechanics of the instrument. Also a special note of appreciation to Mr. Danny Williams in Chicago, baritonist formally with the Cootie Williams Orchestra, with whom I gained invaluable experience while apprenticing several years at band instrument repair and from whom I learned the art of circular breathing. Another good friend who greatly helped to make this album possible was percussionist Sonny Morgan, out of Philadelphia, Pennsylvania, who was recording engineer for this session.

Therefore, to all "who hath an ear," have a pleasant trip through previously uncharted realms.—Pat Patrick 1980

INTERVIEW WITH LA'SHON ANTHONY

On April 20, 2014, I visited with La'Shon Anthony in her home. She is the half sister of Rhonda and Deval who has lived in Chicago all of her life.

La'Shon Anthony: I was raised by my grandmother and grandfather who lived with my aunt and uncle. The very first time I met Rhonda and Deval I did not know they were my brother and sister. Pat brought them over to my home. We stayed in the apartment and visited. The next time I remember I was informed that they were actually my brother and sister. I was introduced to him as my father one day like this, too, but there might have been earlier visits.

Deval and Rhonda lived walking distance from me. As I became older, we would get together. Emily, their mom who was a fantastic person, would also get us all together and take us all places. Easter egg hunts, I remember. As I became a teenager, I would walk over to their place on my own and they would walk over to my place.

Pat did not make a habit of regularly visiting. He did not give me his last name or support me financially. But it was not my place back then to ask something like that. When he had gigs in Chicago, he would call and say he was in town. He'd call and say, "I'd love to get together with you." And we did.

He was extremely disrespectful of my mother in the way he would talk about her to me. Even at an early age I understood, it was not just her fault. Two adults made a conscious decision to have an affair even though he was a married man. So, because of this I dealt with Pat in a civil way, but at a distance. My mother's name was Zenobia Roberts who later took the last name Ali when she married.

The entire situation was a hard pill to swallow. But I never let him know that this bothered me. In introspect now, I wish I had said something before he passed away because this would have given me closure. I never met or got to know some other members of his family—his father and sisters in California. I only knew his sister Sheila and his mother Laverne who both lived in East Moline. Just recently, I have begun speaking with his sister, Darlene Patrick Forest, in California.

There were some visitations during my teens and I did visit Pat once in Queens. During this time, he was married again and I stayed with him for a week. While there, Pat took me to a place called Syncopation. A few of his band members were playing there. He went up on stage and played. I also came back to attend Deval's wedding in New York in 1984.

I knew from reading and from my aunt & uncle that he had played at various clubs in the Chicago area. My aunt told me she and her sister had seen him at these clubs. I later went to see Bob Fosse's *Dancing* when he was on the road with them and playing in the orchestra.

Emily never retaliated with me. She was always gracious. She later moved to Boston but would come back to Chicago to visit and we would get together.

Near the end of his life, I remember visiting Pat in his apartment in East Moline. He told me he would have to leave that apartment and move in with his mother. This was around 1990 or '91. His mother, Laverne, called me and told me of his death, the funeral and I made arrangements to go down there. Emily, Deval, and Rhonda came also.

Hanging in La'Shon's dining room is a large photograph of her father, Pat Patrick, on canvas. She has a wealth of clippings, articles, photographs, and original playbills from the 1970s and 1980s shows that I had not seen. It was a very rich visit.)

· 7 ·

Artistry 1980s and 1990s

I suppose that it would appear to a lot of young people that the world/life of a musician, particularly rock, pop musicians these days is a very glamorous and lucrative life to get into. This may be often true for a white person (with no talent) than for a Black musician with all kinds of abilities to play.

—Pat Patrick, from "Yesterdays, Todays and Tomorrows"

1980s

With the continuing changes in American popular culture tastes and the ways that traditional music venues produced product, including the increased use of electronics and the reduction in numbers of live musicians, the 1980s were difficult for Patrick. He still played with Sun Ra, gigged locally, and travelled some internationally. He still did some recording and performed with some big bands, including Sun Ra, Illinois Jacquet, Mercer Ellington, and Clarke Terry. But the "golden playing era" of gigging that existed in the 1950s, 1960s, and 1970s was over for Pat. In his final days in 1991, living with the knowledge of his leukemia, he moved to his mother's home in East Moline, Illinois. His story comes full circle, and his life ends where it began.

Although the 1960s and 1970s loom huge in memory as the productive decades that many look toward as culturally defining, the 1980s are often lamented in some ways as the loss of innocence and the establishment of a new corporate status quo. Creative freedoms were squeezed. There no longer seemed to be room for radical voices. The 1980s presented new paradigms

Sun Ra Seated with Scores
From the Pat Patrick Archive

Pat Patrick Portrait
From the Pat Patrick Archive

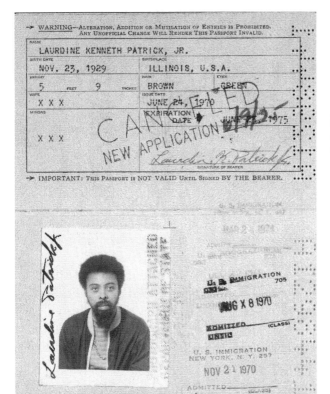

NAME
LAURDINE KENNETH PATRICK, JR.

BIRTH DATE
NOV. 23, 1929

BIRTHPLACE
ILLINOIS, U.S.A.

HEIGHT
5 FEET 9 INCHES

HAIR
BROWN

EYES
GREEN

WIFE
X X X

ISSUE DATE
JUNE 24, 1970

MINORS
X X X

EXPIRATION DATE
JUNE 23, 1975

CANCELLED
NEW APPLICATION

SIGNATURE OF BEARER
Laurdine K. Patrick Jr.

IMPORTANT: THIS PASSPORT IS NOT VALID UNTIL SIGNED BY THE BEARER.

U. S. IMMIGRATION
705
AUG X 8 1970
ADMITTED
UNTIL   (CLASS)

U. S. IMMIGRATION
NEW YORK, N. Y. 257
NOV 2 1 1970
ADMITTED
UNTIL   (CLASS)

Pat Patrick Passport
From the Pat Patrick Archive

SELECTED DISCOVERY

Sun Ra Arkestra –
  "Futuristic Sounds" Savoy Records
  "Magic City" Saturn Records
  "Reflections in Blue" Black Saint
    Records
  "Stay Awake" A&M Records
James Moody –
  "Last Train From Overbrook
    Argo Records
Quincy Jones –
  "Live at Newport '61"
    Mercury/Trip Records
John Coltrane –
  "African Brass" Vols. 1 & II
    Impulse Records
Andrew Hill –
  "One For One" Blue Note Records
Clifford Jordan –
  "Inward Fire" Muse Records
Baritone Saxophone Retinue –
  "Sound Advice" Saturn Records
Leslie Drayton Orchestra –
  "Close Pursuit" Esoteric Records
Johnny Griffin –
  "Big Soul Band" Riverside Records
Graham Monour –
  "Echoes of Prayer" JCOA Records
Jimmy Heath –
  "Really Big" Riverside Records
Sam Jones –
  "Fast Company" Milestone Records
Art Blakey –
  "Golden Boy" Colpix Records
Michael Olatunji –
  "Drums-Drums'Drums" Roulette Records
Roland Kirk –
  "The Case of the Three-Sided Dream"
    Atlantic Records
Mongo Santamaria –
  "Live at Village Gate", Riverside/Battle
    Records
  "Watermelon Man", "Introducing
    La Lupe" Riverside/Battle Records
  "Mongo Explodes" Fantasy Records
Blue Mitchell –
  "A Sure Thing" Riverside Records
Frank Strozier –
  "Long Night" Jazz Land Records
Stanley Cowell –
  "New World" Galaxy Records
Phil Upchurch –
  "Feeling Blue" Milestone Records
Lou Ramirez –
  "Good News" Fania Records
A. K. Salim –
  "Afro-Soul Drum Orgy" Prestige Records

TOURS WITH BROADWAY SHOWS

"The Wiz" – West Coast
"Bubbling Brown Sugar" – Nationally
"Dancin'" – Nationally

TELEVISION APPEARANCES

Maxwell House Coffee commercial
  with Geoffrey Holder
Mike Douglas Show
  with Olatunji
Imamu Baraka Show
  with Baritone Saxophone Retinue
"SOUL" with Letta Mbulu

COMPOSITIONS FOR STAGE PRODUCTIONS

"Kongi's Harvest" written by Wole Soyinka
  produced at
  The Negro Ensemble Co. - N.Y.C.
"The Strong Breed" written
  by Wole Soyinka
  produced by Greenwich
  Mews Theatre - N.Y.C.
"What If It Had Turned Up Heads"
  produced by the
  New Lafayette Theatre - N.Y.C.
"House Party" written by Ed Bullins
  produced by
  American Place Theatre - N.Y.C.
"The Sirens" written by Richard Wesley
  produced at
  Manhattan Theater Club - N.Y.C.

For Further Information Contact:

PAT PATRICK
P.O. Box 15
East Moline, IL 61244
(312) 721-8083

Brochure by ©Marjo Johnson 1990

PAT PATRICK

Saxophonist
Musicologist
Composer

Pat Patrick Resume Brochure
From the Pat Patrick Archive

LAURDINE (PAT) PATRICK, saxophonist, composer, arranger, teacher; comes from Moline, Illinois. He received his first musical training on trumpet from his father and Clark Terry, and was also tutored privately on saxophone and clarinet by Willie Randall of the Earl Hines Orchestra and Professor Johnny Hauser.

He studied with the legendary Captain Walter Dyett at Chicago's DuSable High school from where he graduated with a music scholarship to Florida A & M College in Tallahasse, Florida.

He started his professional career in the late 1940s performing with some of Chicago's living giants such as Lil Armstrong, Muddy Waters, Sun Ra, King Kolax, Gene Ammons, Von Freeman and Red Saunders, to name a few. In the 1950s he worked with such illustrious names as Sammy Davis, Jr., Dinah Washington, Erskine Hawkins, and Nancy Wilson.

In the early 1960s Mr. Patrick moved to New York City and was hired to tour with the James Moody Septet, as well as the orchestras of Quincy Jones and Duke Ellington. By the mid 1960s Mr. Patrick's reputation as a superb player landed him stints as musical director for the Mongo Santamaria band and the Michael Olatunji Afro-American Dance Groups, and gigs with every major performing artist from Thelonius Monk, Billy Taylor and Cal Tjader, to Patti LaBelle, Marvin Gaye and Chuck Jackson.

Mr. Patrick has been a mainstay of the Sun Ra Arkestra since joining the band over 25 years ago, yet he has managed to utilize his musical abilities in every facet of the music field which also includes writing for several stage productions, many of which he was the musical director, acting in workshop productions, and teaching in state-sponsored summer community programs. Among his extensive list of achievements is the formation of the acclaimed "Baritone Saxophone Retinue" which was the first group to feature all baritone saxophones.

His phenomenal musical background as a musician, composer and arranger placed him high in the critics' and readers' polls in Downbeat Magazine in the 1970s, and made him the subject of many feature stories in other major music magazines in the U.S. and Europe.

Despite his ever busy schedule, Mr. Patrick found time to teach in the late 1970s as an Adjunct Professor at the State University of New York, Old Westbury College. Throughout the 1980s he has continued to tour and record with the Sun Ra Arkestra as well as tours with the orchestras of Illinois Jacquet, Mercer Ellington, Lionel Hampton, and Leslie Drayton.

While many of Mr. Patrick's compositions have been recorded by such artists as Clark Terry, Coleman Hawkins, Sun Ra, and Mongo Santamaria, the most widely recorded composition has been "Yeh Yeh" which was used in the movie "Good Morning Vietnam," was a number one hit in England in 1965 and also recorded by Lambert, Hendricks, and Bavan, The Three Sounds, Baby Cortez, Gerald Wilson, Georgie Fame, and Jerry Fielding and the Hollywood Brass.

Pat Patrick Resume Brochure
From the Pat Patrick Archive

Pat Patrick, Charles Davis Interview with Amiri Baraka
From the Pat Patrick Archive

Pat Patrick with Duke Ellington
From the Pat Patrick Archive

Pat Patrick with Clark Terry
From the Pat Patrick Archive

Pat Patrick Portrait
From the Pat Patrick Archive

Pat Patrick Performing
From the Pat Patrick Archive

Pat Patrick Composing
From the Pat Patrick Archive

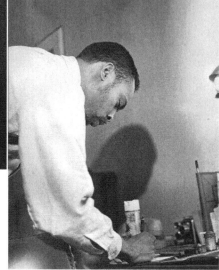

Pat Patrick Baritone Retinue
From the Pat Patrick Archive

Pat Patrick Performing
From the Pat Patrick Archive

1950s Dance Club
From the Pat Patrick Archive

Sun Ra in Mexico
From the Pat Patrick Archive

Pat Patrick Playing the Flute
From the Pat Patrick Archive

Pat Patrick Performing
From the Pat Patrick Archive

Sun Ra Performing
From the Pat Patrick Archive

Pat Patrick with Thelonius Monk
From the Pat Patrick Archive

that sounded and felt corporate. Older jazz musicians of Pat Patrick's generation were no longer the "in group." Although many were working, the pace
of the work was much slower than it had been. Much of the presence that
defined music in decades past resonated differently now.

In a conversation with Pat Patrick's great friend and collaborator,
saxophonist Charles Davis, we asked him, "When did things change?" He
recalled,

> The gigs didn't go away that fast, because there was still Miles and Monk,
> Sonny Rollins. . . . The music was still strong. But when they died, that's
> when it got stranger. Miles switched over, Coltrane passed, and Sonny
> went to Calypso, then the stuff went, ahh. So things just happened.
> . . . I remember my wife and I went out to see a show out in Valley Forge.
> They got us up into some seats where the band was playing. I peeped
> over and there was nothing there but the drummer. He was playing with
> [prerecorded] tracks. So this was in the 1980s. So I asked him, "What
> happened to the rest of the band?" . . . They just put the stuff on tape and
> he was the only live musician. So these kinds of gimmicks came along,
> and it's just like the auto industry. "You can go now." Machines don't go
> on breaks, and they don't ask for a raise.

Cultural patterns change work patterns. And the work patterns dictate music
and entertainment in our culture. What's interesting, too, is watching these
shifts and noting how musicians like Pat Patrick related and responded to
these major societal changes.

Pat expressed concern in his writings about the commercial "conspiracy"
early in his workings in the industry. By the 1970s, he had seen "the changes"
as a player; as a recording artist with publishing rights and royalties, he had
produced shows, written grants for support of his art, and was right in the
middle of the stylistic shifts that went from jazz to a much more aggressive
support system for mainstream popular music. He witnessed directly the effects: the gigs were not as frequent and the listeners were now turned on and
tuned into a new beat. He writes,

> That is the story of what has been happening to our music to this very
> day. So what is the season that is being claimed as their own by some of
> these assimilations of jazz? Simple: it has proven to be a highly commercial
> product.
>   The original sounds that have had so much to do with the founda-
> tion and the formation of our culture have through the ages been used
> and misused for all sorts of purposes other than what the music was/is
> intended for. It seems that the music often heard these days, no matter
> how one thinks he enjoys it (it too often reflects sex and or lovemaking),

is not contributing enough toward a greater awareness for Black folks. Perhaps the world would not be in a chaotic state if natural orders of laws had been followed. This is not to say that notable or worthy music has not come along in the past. But too often, as in the case of the Black folks, many, many benefits derived from his work have been diverted away from him and his people by something or other. This is no accident but rather a carefully worked out conspiracy.

Those cultural shifts and the "many benefits" that have been "diverted away" from the artist are precisely what Patrick was responding and reacting to. We see this in his family relations, artistic commitments, and ideological views. We see how these shifts affect his income as a musician and how this later equates to his creative output. The bubble of the protective arsenal of Sun Ra, musicianship loyalties, and their beliefs in their art was to come against a new cultural popular framework for which all had to be prepared. These are the forces that impacted Pat Patrick's life.

As Amiri Baraka explains in "Essay from Digging, the Afro-American Soul of American Classical Music,"

> The point is that if the music is to create with its direct beauty the social economic aesthetic intellectual material reflection of its expressive aesthetic presence, then new work has to be done by all of us concerned for one reason or another. . . . We must begin to see the music, not only its fundamental creation, but all the elements, aspects, individuals and organizations, as part of one thing.[1]

PAT PATRICK'S RESUME AND LETTER

Resume

- April 6, 7, 1983, Egypt, Cairo, Alexandria
- August 5, 6, 1983, Charles Davis and the Baritone Saxophone Retinue, Jazz Cultural Heritage Theater, 368 Eighth Avenue, near Twenty-Eighth (sponsored by the National Endowment of the Arts)
- 1983, Renue, Jazz Culture Theater, Chelsea
- 1983, Goethe Institute, Cairo, starring Pat Patrick
- 1983, Recording with Leslie Drayton, Close Pursuit, Los Angeles, Esoteric Recordings
- 1984, Recording with Leslie Drayton Orchestra featuring Barbara Morrison, Los Angeles, Esoteric Recordings

- 1984, Recording with Terry Adams and Friends, Tribute to Thelonious Monk, New York
- 1985, Sweet Saturday Night, August 6–10, Lincoln Center Outdoor Concerts
- 1986, Egypt
- May 18, 1987, Pavilion, with Sun Ra, North Hollywood, California, "Night Watch," TV show in D.C., Sun Ra
- 1988, Recorded with Sun Ra Arkestra, *Stay Awake*, New York, A&M Recordings

Letter

8/26/1983

Hi Mom,

Got your last letter with the stuff from American Express. Thanks. Just thought I'd send you this stuff to bring you up to date on what I'm doing. These reviews are from the *New York Times* paper. The card is from the club that I'm working at and we start two nights a week in September. It's just me and a guitar, so it's real easy and they treat us real nice too. One of the owners is a brother. I wish Gene Edwards was in town. He could work with me there, although the white boy I've got is good. I've known him for a long time and we get along well together.

I may be getting a phone soon, so I'll call you when I do. I'm looking forward to Deval coming to town to live in the next week or so. I'll keep you posted. Say Hi to all the kids and folks for me. Stay sweet. Hope you're feeling music better now.

Take care,
Yours, Pat

GETTING STARTED: WORDS WITH DEVAL AND RHONDA

In his biography, *A Reason to Believe: Lessons from an Improbable Life*, Deval Patrick writes,

In the years immediately following the blowout with my father, our relationship slowly began to mend. . . . The summer before my third year of law school, 1982, I worked at a law firm in Washington, D.C. I turned twenty-five that July, and on my birthday, my father happened to be playing in a local jazz club called Pigfoot and invited me to join him.

I arrived near the end of the first set, just before the break, and my father was playing the saxophone, jamming with a skilled quartet. . . . He took the microphone and said to the crowd, "It's my son's birthday, and I want to play this next tune for him." He played an old standard, "I Can't Get Started." He looked me straight in the eye while he played, long and soulfully, full of regret and longing all at once. I gazed right back at him, knowing what he was trying to say: "[Son,] Life is too short to go on like this, let's find a way to come together." It was clear how much we both wanted simple understanding.

When Diane and I got married in 1984, my father organized his friends to play at our wedding. This ensured that we had good music, as we lacked the funds for a band. . . . My father took to staying with us in Brooklyn for long periods when he was in between concert tours or on the outs with his girlfriend. Even when he wasn't living with us, he was a part of our lives, and he was eager to play his part as father-in-law.

Diane was pregnant. . . . I went by her favorite Italian restaurant to pick up a special dinner to take to the hospital. . . . I stood on a midtown corner trying to hail a cab. My father was then driving part time a business tycoon's gray limousine, and he miraculously spotted me.

He pulled up, told me to hop in the back, and asked me where I needed to go. . . . I told him to take me to Lenox Hill Hospital, where I was going to have dinner with his new granddaughter.

By the time Katherine had grown into a sassy toddler, he would come to our house in Milton and dote on two precious little girls. He gave them fifes and little flutes and played the sax for them while they danced around our front hall. . . . How fitting that the finest gig of his life was that of a grandfather.[2]

In an interview we conducted with Rhonda Patrick-Sigh, she stated,

I remember him calling, and there was an incident with me in Chicago, living right off Lake Shore Drive. A guy broke in on me. He broke in all the apartments. He kicked my door off. I was living with my mother at this time, as roommates. I took out a gun, a little gun we had, and I hid in the closet. I tried to pull the trigger, but it didn't go off. He shot at me, and I fainted, but he ran out. They picked this guy up. My dad was so upset about that. He invited all of us out to California. He was traveling with *Bubbling Brown Sugar* or Bob Fosse's *Dancin'*, I'm not sure which one. So the end of January that year we went out there. By this time, Pat's father had married a Mexican woman, and they had children. So we all got together and had a family reunion.

This was his way to get me out of Chicago. And he knew what he was doing because sure enough, it was 70 below wind chill factor back in Chicago. But in LA it was 70-plus and the sun was out every day.

I said, "Yes, it is time," and I moved that year to California.

We had a relationship. That was strategic on his part. In the later 1980s, he found out he had leukemia. During this period, I got married.

We got our first house and he came out to see his grandchild, Bianca. She was around three years old, maybe my son was born, 1986, 1987. Pat got sick in the bathroom while he was visiting us in San Diego. He went into the bathroom, stumbled, and that's when he shared he was battling with leukemia. This brings us up until 1990 or so.

We would visit Deval twice a year in Boston. We were walking along with Pat. He got sick and fainted so they rushed him to Mass General Hospital.

He decided to move to back home to East Moline to live with my grandmother, and I would assume nothing musically was going on, major, then.

I do remember him in the later years prior to this, coming to San Diego, too, and he ended up playing at a local gig with some friends, Jeanie and Jimmy Cheatham. They were friends who lived there. They had a weekly gig going, lots of jazz. They were in charge of the local jazz scene. They were really good friends of Pat's, and he would play with them, jam sessions. He was always finding something to get involved in musically. Sun Ra was touring then.

We drove about an hour to see him, my grandfather and my daughter. Bianca at this time was playing a piccolo flute my grandfather gave her.

This was about 1986. My dad was playing other instruments, too. I saw him play piano and something else. He was mixing it up. Those different gigs he would get involved with allowed us to get together, to see him, the band, hang out. He would call a few times.

The last time I remember hearing his voice was New Year's Eve, December 31, 1991, on the day he died.

He called my brother's house; that's where everybody was. My brother, my mother, we were all there, in Boston. I hadn't moved there yet. It was a good-bye call. There wasn't anything said, I didn't know it was a good-bye call. I didn't realize he was saying good-bye until I found out he passed the next day. He called from East Moline.

This is the hard part about this call. My mom and Pat, they had such a destructive relationship. Even on this day, she rushed me off the phone with him. She had both her kids there, her grandkids there, and I guess she saw this phone call as a "downer."

I'm sure that's the way she looked at it. It was her way of protecting us. She made us get off the telephone. But that was their relationship. Because she rushed me off the phone, I didn't get to spend enough time with him. That's what hurts me. He was his normal uplifting self. He wasn't saying anything but, "I love you—take care of yourself." Then, she rushes me off the phone, and that was the last time we talked.

My emotion flares up because I'm so angry about this. I think she felt like it was going to bring me down, change everybody's mood, and we wouldn't have harmony. This was not an expected call. That was the last time I heard his voice.

INTERVIEWS WITH BAND MEMBERS MARSHAL ALLEN, DANNY THOMPSON, AND CHARLES DAVIS

In preparation for a concert to be held at Berklee College of Music in February 2014, in celebration of Sun Ra's one hundredth birthday, we met with three surviving members of the Sun Ra band: Marshall Allen, Danny Thompson, and Charles Davis. We brought Deval, the governor of Massachusetts, and his sister Rhonda Patrick-Sigh onstage and made them both honorary members of the Arkestra. We had a chance to hang out and interview the guys about Sun Ra and Pat in those years. We talked about the members' move from Chicago, landing in New York, moving to Philly, workings and gigs, the state of things, and again the general feeling of family, loyalty, respect, and the love for the music the whole crew embodied. Great musicians!

Bill Banfield: What was it like to work with Sun Ra?

Danny Thompson: It was an event. You'd never know what to expect from hour to hour. Working with Sun Ra was fantastic. I'll tell you a story. We were living in New York, 1967. Sun Ra was living on 48 East Third Street, and there were about ten dudes in this two-bedroom apartment. We were taking shifts sleeping. Pat was staying over on Fifth Street.

Sun Ra at that time had three drummers onstage on some gigs, four bass players, with piano, the whole band was in front of the stage. There was no place to sit at Slugs. We would go from 9 p.m., 'til 3 or 4 a.m., no breaks. The only time we could go to the bathroom was during Clifford Jarvis's drum breaks, who would take a half-hour drum solo. That was our cue.

Bill Banfield: Is the devotion of this kind of thing due to the music or was it due to Sun Ra?

Charles Davis: Well, there is no break in this. If you were devoted to Sun Ra, you were devoted to the music, or the other way [around]. You had to have this because it was so intense. The discipline he had you in. You had to have both. You come back, you leave. I had to take a leave of absence for five years. He was like five bosses in one, and he told you ten different things. He was like that. It wasn't easy.

Bill Banfield: In 1968, 1970, what was the money like? How did you eat?

Charles Davis: Oh, with Sun Ra, you were going to eat, because he liked to eat. You'd hear the lecture, you'd get cussed out, but you were going to eat. Or he would cook the moon stew. [All laugh.]

Bill Banfield: What was the regular pay like?

Marshall Allen: I was in the "house band." I lived with Sun Ra. My pay was always short. But I had food. I could eat, and I had a place to stay. We got short money, "don't ask" money. If you needed something, you just ask. There were people in the house band, then there were people who came in for gigs. They got paid. When Sun Ra was on the road, and he had lots of money, then he would share. Then there was some gigs, "Don't ask." The people who stayed on Morton Street, they'd eat, and sometimes he would pay people not to play. If he had some money, he would pay. It was the whole package. You were sincere about the whole package. But you never went hungry.

Bill Banfield: Marshall, your dad actually owned the Philly house on Morton Street and sold the house to Sun. Right?

Marshall Allen: Well, Sun Ra needed a place to stay, so I told my father to sell the house to Sun Ra. And I think he sold it to Sun Ra for $2.

Danny Thompson: We were paying $90 a month. Nobody moved like Sun Ra moved. He took two years to move from New York. We would go every day for two years, driving back and forth from New York to Philly. We had stuff everywhere! Me, John Gilmore, Marshall, Jackson came a year later. The band came down slowly. Sun Ra was getting the rooms ready. He would fix the rooms to "your vibrations." This went on for two years, 1968 and 1969.

Bill Banfield: The house band. Charles, how do you go in and out of this?

Charles Davis: See I started with Sun Ra, back in Chicago. That's the understanding I had, I could go in and out.

Bill Banfield: Pat was able to break out of this. How did that work, in and out?

Charles Davis: Well, Pat had steady, other jobs.

Marshall Allen: You were never out of the band once you were in it.

Danny Thompson: Pat was working in all the Broadway shows. He had a transistor radio and a small portable TV in rehearsals. He never missed a note of the music, or the sports—baseball game, watching football onstage and playing the parts, and never missing a note. Pat was amazingly accomplished. I didn't realize how heavy this cat was. Like Duke had Harry Carney, Sun Ra had Pat. This musician was a true master. This musician was an artist in the true sense of the word. His music and solos were special.

I will never forget working at the Five Spot in New York City, sitting in between Pat Patrick and Charles Davis. The energy and the vibe rising from these two masters was out of this world. For me sitting there, it was like a fire had come over me, and in order not two burn up, I had to become a flame, maybe not as big as the "nine-alarm fire" as Pat, Charles, John Gilmore, Marshall Allen, or Sun Ra, but burn nonetheless. *Space Is the Place!*

Bill Banfield: Did the gigs change? Did you feel the switch in the music culture in the 1980s?

Marshall Allen: Sun Ra was doing so many things, and Sun Ra was so far ahead of the styles that when it changed, he was already doing that.

Bill Banfield: Did the work shift?

All together: Noooooo!

Marshall Allen: We were working in the band, but we had our work in Europe. Sometimes, as many as twenty-seven people for three months. That was unheard of. But we were all working.

Bill Banfield: What else do you remember about the gigging?

Charles Davis: Pat was always working during the 1970s.

Marshall Allen: It all started in about 1960. We took a gig, tour in Canada with the small band out of Chicago, and on the way back we got stranded in a car. Ronnie Boykins, bass player's car, was hit by a cab. And so we decided to just stay in New York, try and make it there while he waited for the insurance money. It took almost a year to get the insurance pay. We ended up just staying there. Then Charles, Pat, all the guys joined. We played in the Village for dinner and transportation. We played the coffeehouses. That's why most of the band had to do other things.

So in order for us to work, we played coffeehouses in the Village. You'd get car fare home and back and a good meal.

Bill Banfield: Let's talk about the respect level of Pat. He was highly respected. How did Gilmore, Coltrane feel about Patrick?

Danny Thompson: Gilmore was a force of nature in himself. These were humble guys; they weren't, "We bad!" No, people would encourage you. These were the kind of players they were. They would pump you up, give you something to go by. They were "other kinds" of musicians. Sun Ra wouldn't care though if you could play or not. He would just get you to playing. Sun Ra would say, "This is a creator's band." He would put in who he wanted.

Bill Banfield: Let's talk about Pat. What he was doing in the 1970s and 1980s?

Marshall Allen: Every gig he had, he'd give me another gig, Oluntunja, shows. He would always come by and give me gigs. As long as I knew him, he couldn't make all the gigs, so he would pass them along because he couldn't make them all. In the 1970s, it was the same thing. We'd travel.

Pat was on a lot of those gigs, the tours. He played alto and bass more in the later years.

Charles Davis: Sun Ra was funny. If he was mad at you for any reason he might "do things." If he was mad at Pat, if he was upset, Sun Ra would put me on baritone sax. And so once I replaced Pat. That's how I started playing baritone. Pat was in and out. He never lived with us. He was doing a lot of things we don't know about too.

Bill Banfield: The *Saturday Night Live* performance. Tell me about this.

Danny Thompson: It was a good payday! We got paid several times. We did the gig. We were for three months in Mexico City. Pat was there. Then we came to New York. We rehearsed. It was live, then the we just did it. Even years later we got checks, because John Belushi and them were playing that "Cheeseburger, Cheeseburger" thing.

On the road we used to play cards. This would keep us out of trouble. We played Tonk. Pat called it, "Foun't" or found out. The next day, you would wear your winnings. On the bus, everywhere, me, Marshall, John, Pat. It was like a family.

Bill Banfield: Did you buy into the Sun Ra theology?

Charles Davis: Of course, we saw it was real. You could see it happening. His philosophy, his being was about this music. His spiritual thing, cosmology. He wasn't looking for a righteous man. He said a righteous man is a laughing-stock. A lot of his beliefs are still coming true. In *Joyful Noise*, he's in front of the White House. He said, "The equations are wrong here. There's no Black House. You have a White House here. Where is the Black house?" Well, now we have Obama. Sun Ra's stuff comes true. He was talking about a man on the moon before they even landed. He had insights, and insights on music.

Family members Deval, Rhonda, La'Shon, made honorary members of their father's home band, the Sun Ra Arkestra.

• 8 •

Works Closure

Many times, when we see our children unable or unwilling to sit still and be attentive and listen when in class or an assembly or other group gathering where there is something to be learned, it is because their power of concentration has been destroyed. This is the type of power we as Black people should be most concerned with. At this date in time, because today's youth is definitely the future generation, they must be equipped if they expect to survive under the advanced pressure.

—Pat Patrick, from unfinished article on education

Pat Patrick is the "musician's working musician" extraordinaire. It is easy to make such claims for the work of an artist we admire. But it is quite another thing when you have the work documented with evidence that shows an impact on culture and a trajectory that inspires the way forward. The musicians from the period in which Pat Patrick worked moved our musical paths forward. There really are few other periods that exemplify the explosion of variety and greatness in popular musical culture like those found in the 1960s and 1970s.

Patrick was also a "race man." He strove to use his art to improve the race and to uplift. The quotation that begins this section is an example of his ideas about education and self-improvement. His timeline shows how prolific he was and how hard he worked. His timeline also reveals his commitment to making the country better and to improving the value placed on the African American cultural heritage.

TIMELINE

1949 First Annual NAACP Midnight Show, the Regal, one week in orchestra with Nat King Cole, Cootie Williams, Dinah Washington, and Illinois Jacket

July 1949 Pat Patrick with the Otis Welch Orchestras, Bop City at the Rose Bowl Ballroom every Friday beginning July 29, 1949

September 15, 1950 George Tolbert Review with Pat Patrick and Barry Sax, Big Progressive Club

1951 Famous Door sessions

1952 With Earl Fatha Hines, St. Louis

1953 With Horace Henderson, New Trianon Ballroom, Chicago

June 24, 26, 1954 Horace Henderson and his orchestra, Sixty-Second Street and Cottage Grove Avenue

July 1954 Recorded with Horace Henderson, Chicago, WIND broadcast, Trianon Ballroom

January 30, 1955 Pat Patrick and His All Stars, Carven High School B Auditorium

January 1956 Recorded with Billie Hawkins and the Sun Ra Arkestra, Chicago, Heartbeat Recordings

February–May 1956 Recorded with Sun Ra and His Arkestra, Saturn Recordings

October 1956 Recorded with Andrew Hill Combo, Chicago, Ping Recordings

1957–1959 Recordings with Sun Ra Archestra, Chicago

1959 *The Cry of Jazz* is released, featuring the Sun Ra Arkestra

December 1959 With Richard Evans Trio

1960–1961 Worked with James Moody Septet, World's Fair in New York City; recorded with Johnny Griffith, the Big-Soul Johnny Griffin Orchestra with Clark Terry, Pat Patrick, Charles Davis, Julien Priester

May 24, 31, June 3, 1960 New York, Riverside Recordings

June 24, 28, 1960 Recorded with Jimmy Heath *Really Big!* Jimmy Health Orchestra, New York

Recorded with John Coltrane, *Africa Brass*, the John Coltrane Quartet, Englewood Cliffs, New Jersey, Impulse Recordings

June 1961 Duke Ellington

July 3, 1961 Quincy Jones Orchestra, Live at Newport, Newport, Rhode Island

August 15, 1961 Recorded with Sam Jones, New York, Riverside Recordings

September 12, 1961 Recorded with Frank Stokier Quartet, New York, Jazzland Recordings

October 1961 Recorded with Sun Ra Arkestra, New York, Savoy, Saturn Recordings

1962 Recorded with Mongo Santamaria, Live the Black Hawk, San Francisco, California

1962 Recorded with Sun Ra Arkestra

June 25, 1962 Recorded with Cannonball Adderley and his orchestra, New York, Riverside Recordings

July 9, 11, 1962 Recorded with Mongo Santamaria, Go Mongo, New York, Milestone Recordings

October 1962 Recorded with Sun Ra Arkestra, New York, Savoy, Saturn Recordings

December 17, 1962 Recorded with Phil Diaz, Cal Jader, Mongo Santamaria (Watermelon Man), New York; performed with Clarke Terry, Coleman Hawkins, Lambert and Hendricks

1963 Recorded with Sun Ra Arkestra

February 18–19, 1963 Recorded with Mongo Santamaria, New York, Mongo Records; Patrick's "Yeh Yeh" later becomes a hit

1964 Recorded with Sun Ra Arkestra

1964 Served as musical director for Afro American Dance Group

1964 Performed in the New York World's Fair with Babatunde Olatunji, African Pavilion

Spring 1964 Recorded with Mongo Santamaria, Mongo at Village Gate, New York

October 8, 1964 Recorded with A. K. Salim, Afro Soul Drum Orgy, New York

December 31, 1964 Recorded with Pharoah Sanders and Black Harold, New York, Saturn Recordings

1965 Toured colleges with Sun Ra

1965–1966 Recorded with Sun Ra Arkestra

1966 Sun Ra and His Solar Arkestra (with Marshall Allen, Charles Davis and John Gilmore), played "space lute"

1966–1969 Recorded with Sun Ra and His Solar Arkestra Visits Planet Earth, Saturn Records. Performed with Montego Joe, Machito, Marvin Gaye, Kim Weston, Marvelettes, Billy Taylor, Chuck Jackson, Kako Ysu, Patty Labelle and the Blue Bells; performed at numerous East and West Coast colleges with Sun Ra and two days of concerts at Carnegie Hall; performed with the Jean-Leon Destine Haitian Dance Company, the Nigerian Highlife Orchestras; composed music for plays by Nigerian playwright Wole Soyinka (*The String Breed*, Greenwich Village, October 1967, and *Kongi's Harvest*), jockey on WBAI-FM radio doing shows on roots of jazz, the music of Sun Ra

June 21, 1966 Recorded with Freedie McCoy, Funk Drops, New York, Prestige Recordings

1967 Recorded with Sun Ra Arkestra

1967 Served as music director for Wole Soyinka play, *The Trial of Broke Jero*

September 12, 1967 Recorded with Phil Upchurch, New York, Actuel Recordings

September 12, 1967, 1968 Recorded with Phil Upchurch, Feeling Blue, Milestone Recordings

1968 Served as music director for Wole Soyinka play, *Strong Breed*

1968 Featured as *BMI Magazine*'s "Musician of Note"

1968 Toured colleges with Sun Ra, performed at Newport Jazz festival and Boston Globe festival

1968 Recorded with Sun Ra Arkestra

April 1968 Recognized as *Record World*'s "All-Star Band/New Artist"

1969 Recorded with Sun Ra Arkestra

1969 Recorded with Olatunji, New York, Roulette Recordings

1969 Toured colleges with Sun Ra, performed at Newport Jazz festival and Boston Globe festival

January 16, 1970 Recorded with Andrew Hill, New York, Bluenote recordings, Pat Patrick with Charles Tolliver, Bennie Maupin, Ron Cater, Paul Motian

February 19, 1970 Pat Patrick joined the Thelonious Monk Ensemble, Village Vanguard

June 6–June 13, 1970 Music for *Guerra*

1971–1972 Winner *Downbeat Magazine* established talent poll

1972 Recorded the album *Space Is the Place* with the Sun Ra Archestra, on ABC/Impulse Records

1972 Founded Baritone Saxophone Retinue Band with Charles Davis

1972 Became music editor of *Black Theatre Magazine*

1972 Music director for J. E. Games play *Sometimes a Hard Head Makes a Soft Behind*

1973 Music director for Paul Harrison, *Requiem for Brother X*

1973 Adjunct professor, State University of New York, Old Westbury College

February, March 1973 TV debut, Imaru Baraka, Black Newark

April 4, 1974 Recorded with Clifford Thorton and the Jazz Composers Orchestra, New York, JCOA Recording

April 11, 1974 Recorded with Grachan Moncur, Jazz Composers Orchestra Association

March 9, 1975 Recorded with Robert Northern, Brother Asah, New York, Divine Recordings

May 14, 1975 Recorded with Rahsaan Roland Kirk, Atlantic Recordings
1976 Sam Wooding, Bicentennial Jazz Vistas, New York, Twin Sign Recording
1976 Famous Ballroom, Baltimore, Maryland, with Sun Ra
June 25, 1976 Jazz Composers Orchestra
July 9, 1976 Recorded Live at Montreux: Sun Ra and His Arkestra; performed at Montreux Jazz festival
March 1977 Gig with Renuite Ensemble
April 5, 1977 Recorded with Clifford Jordan and his band, Inward Fire, Muse Recordings
June 29–30, August 1, October 27–28, 1977 Recorded with Bobby Watson, New York
1978–1979 Henry Street Settlement, New Federal Theater, with Amiri Baraka
November 1978 Stanley Cowell, New World, Berkeley, California, Galaxy Recordings
June 23, 1979 Awarded Music Excellence Award, Consortium of Jazz Organizations

SUMMARY

As a point of summary about these evidentiary pieces, Pat was a saxophonist, multi-wind player, arranger, composer, music director, and theater works producer. Between 1960 and 1985, Pat performed or recorded with the Duke Ellington and Quincy Jones orchestras, Thelonious Monk, Mongo Santamaria, Nat King Cole, James Moody, Eric Dolphy, Art Blakely, Marvin Gaye, Patti LaBelle, Billy Taylor, Della Reese, Cannonball Adderley, Ahmad Jamal, Eartha Kitt, Benny Golson, Pearl Bailey, Louis Bellson, Rahsaan Roland Kirk, Bobby Watson, Clifford Jordan, David Murray, Stanley Cowell, Bunny Briggs, Willie Dixon, Earl Hines, Sil Austin, Cootie Williams, Cab Calloway, the Nicholas Brothers, Blue Mitchell, Willie Bobo, Babs Gonzales, Barry Harris, Clark Terry Big Band, Ernie Wilkins, Sam Wooding Orchestra, Jimmy Heath, Johnny Griffin, Andrew Hill, Nat Adderley, Leon Thomas, Louis Ramirez, Percy Heath, Buddy Defranco, the Machito Orchestra, Hilton Rutz, Sam Jones Orchestra, Philly Joe Jones, Gigi Gryce, Jean-Leon Destine Dance Group, and more. He laid down the bottom on the baritone saxophone with the indefinable Sun Ra Arkestra for thirty-five-plus years from 1952 to 1988.

Taking yet another note of departure on this journey, his daughter Rhonda Patrick-Sigh concludes, "Well, we know that music was his first love. And he served that community well. Not only through physical talent but how he tried to bring Black culture together through his philosophy, his wisdom and understanding of how the Black community could be better through music and each other. He wanted to 'better' the culture."

As a "race man"—that is, as a child of the generation who aspired toward making good on the promises of freedom, equality, and meaningful struggle for progress forward—Pat lived well and succeeded.

Pat Patrick focused his music on his concern for the culture and the role of raising it up, seeing that the next generations took it even further. This is clear in his writings, in his reflections, and in his music. It was also part of his teaching to his peers and his students. He imbued in his children his deep belief in the worth of music.

Pat Patrick's story is an American story. It is the tale of a musician who sought for meaning, who struggled, who had success, and who made mistakes. In many ways, his story reveals not only great musicianship, but it sheds light on the larger scope of human expression. His story helps us understand American history, especially the turbulent period of the 1960s and 1970s, when so much was rebooted and new directions were set. This view into the life of Pat Patrick helps us to understand him and to understand ourselves a little bit more.

· 9 ·

Interviews with Charles Davis, Richard Evans, and Pat Patrick

CHARLES DAVIS

We interviewed several of Pat's associates, friends who knew him as a musician. We heard a bit from Charles Davis earlier; here we have a detailed discussion with him. We had the pleasure of spending an afternoon with Charles on March 13, 2013, at his home in New York. Charles was seventy-nine at the time and had been living in the same home for more than thirty years. Born in Mississippi and raised in Chicago, Charles graduated from DuSable High, the same high school that Pat attended. Charles also studied at the Chicago School of Music. During the 1950s, he played with Billie Holiday and Ben Webster, Sun Ra and Dinah Washington. He then performed, recorded, and toured with Kenny Dorham.

Like Patrick, Sun Ra, and many others, Charles moved to New York, but a little earlier than they did, arriving in 1959. His work as a musician has not stopped. His list of musical associations, particularly in jazz, is tremendous. In the 1960s, he performed and recorded with Elvin Jones, Jimmy Garrison, Illinois Jacquet, Freddie Hubbard, Johnny Griffin, Steve Lacy, Ahmad Jamal, Blue Mitchell, Erskine Hawkins, John Coltrane, and Clifford Jordan, among others.

He was the cofounder, along with Pat Patrick, of the Retinue Baritone Saxophone Ensemble, a completely unique ensemble of all baritone saxes and rhythm support. Like Patrick, in addition to playing in the Sun Ra Arkestra, he also played with the Clarke Terry Orchestra and toured with the Duke Ellington Orchestra under the direction of Mercer Ellington. He also recorded and toured in Europe and Japan with the Clifford Jordan Big Band.

In the 1990s, known as a New York musician who some might call a "walking library," he served as musical librarian for Spike Lee's *Mo' Better Blues*, a movie about a character dedicated to being a jazz musician. Davis has made eight of his own albums and is featured on more than one hundred recordings.

For Davis, musicians do the things musicians do, which is to make music and not necessarily to try to make history. Movements, ideas, and conventions may grow out of the lives of musicians, but, according to Charles Davis, they are not consciously constructing a historical line. Even when it came to framing his friend Pat Patrick in this "certain way," Charles was matter of fact. He didn't want to reveal things that he thought were unnecessary. And so several of the ideas mentioned, such as the tenor of the times or dealing with the shifts in popular music trends or the daily hustle of keeping busy as a musician, shifting from gig to gig, all became something that Pat did, as any musician would, in order to continue working over a long career.

The life a working, gigging musician has reveals a kind of "nomad for the notes" lifestyle that shapes the direction of the professional paths—many times unstable, yet unstoppable—of many musicians. Charles, though a different musician often on a different path than Pat, provides a window into the life of the New York working musician of the period. What came to his mind and what he shared was, "I want you tell the truth about my friend Pat, who was a great guy and a great musician. He was my friend, a guy who inspired me to play baritone sax and sold me my first baritone. We, as friends, we just watched each other throughout all the years, even up to the last year of his death." Charles saw Pat in the last year of his life in Chicago. This is someone who knew Patrick in his early days in Chicago and through the years. And that's another thing you take away from this: that the musicians are musicians for life.

They work, they live, they have children, and they support each other. They live for the music. That is a beautiful thing. When you walk the life of somebody, retracing his or her steps, this kind of overall picture is helpful. The smaller steps are not always the definitive nuggets of truth that help you to understand what the life or the music was about. The truth comes from tracing relationships to see connections. It's the broader themes that help us to flesh out the narrative and see, in light, the deeper truths.

Bill Banfield: Charles, could you start describing your life, moving forward to you knowing Pat Patrick?

Charles Davis: Well, I was born in Goodman, Mississippi, May 20, 1933. And at the age of three, I moved out to Chicago. My father got a job on Milwaukee Road as a Pullman porter. That got us there. He went first, then me and my mother came up later, 1935, 1936. Black folks moved from all over, Mississippi, Alabama. One of the things that I was blessed with being in Chicago was there was always music around of some sort. You know, with the bands, Count Basie, Duke Ellington, Lionel Hampton.

Growing up there as a kid, living on the south side, I remember seeing Gene Ammonds rehearsing in the garage. You know, when you are a little kid, you don't know what you are seeing or who these people are until later on. I remember my mother taking me to the Regal Theater to see Jay Mcshann, with Charley Parker in the band. I remember him playing a solo, and he tore the house up. This had to be in 1939 or 1940. Then it came to me later who he was, but I had already seen him in Chicago as a little kid. I was always fascinated from then on with saxophones.

Well, then, later on, growing up, I got influenced by Lester Young, Coleman Hawkins, and the guys playing around Chicago: Johnny Griffin, Vaughn Freeman. These were the older musicians. Then I saw Pat, who ran in different bands. I fell in love with the baritone from hearing Leo Parker, then that led me to Pat Patrick. And I started getting interested in the baritone sax. I bought my first baritone from him, and I learned to play it.

Bill Banfield: Did you go to Dusable High? What was it like?

Charles Davis: That's a whole other story in itself. Many of the guys I named went to Dusable.

There were guys just coming through there all the time, so many big guys. At one time, Captain Dyett [the band director] had taught Nat Cole and Dinah Washington, Richard Davis, and Richard Evans. Then I got in Sun Ra's band, and we were playing; we were "swinging." I mean *space* was not the place then, not in 1956.

Bill Banfield: Tell me about Sun Ra, playing in the orchestra over the years. How was he to work under as a musician?

Charles Davis: He was always Sun Ra, you know.

Bill Banfield: And his beliefs?

Charles Davis: You asked about his musicianship. But with his philosophy, I'd argue with him about that. "No," I'd say, "I don't believe that shit." Sun Ra was unique. He'd keep guys out of the army. He'd go and play at the insane asylum for people. He was that type of person. He would rehearse all day and then not play that music. How about that one? Me, Danny Thompson, and Pat, we had three baritones in the band then, with Sun Ra in the 1970s. We played for three weeks, then, at the Five Spot, then I went out with them on the road.

I remember traveling with him 1975. We went across the country. We'd play a gig, and I looked up and the band would be bigger! People would just be up there. Go to the next gig, they'd be some other people. People would just want to be around him. We would rehearse all day on some stuff, and then he wouldn't play it.

Bill Banfield: What kind of person was Pat?

Charles Davis: I mean, like I told you, he was a nice guy. He was my friend. When you're dealing with friends as musicians, that's it. He was always hustling and working at a repair shop in Chicago. That's when the kids were little. He brought the kids around. I knew his sister and the wife.

Bill Banfield: Did you move in 1960 with them to New York? And how was the gigging life there for musicians?

Charles Davis: I didn't move with them. I got there in 1959 on my own. I had just left Dinah Washington. I went out to California with Clifford Jordan. I couldn't stand it, then I went on back to Chicago, then on to New York on a gig with Kenny Durham.

I worked with him for a few years here in New York. Our gig life was fine. We went in, came out again, and came in for a few more months. Nightly gigs.

Money was different then, not as much as it is now. But that was what was happening. I wasn't making a hell of a lot of money, but we were making a little change.

I remember Vernel Fourney, saying he raised a family working on gigs living on the south side of Chicago, and he never worked on the north side. That's the way gigs were. My first gig was with Billie Holiday in Chicago at Budland in1956. I stayed in there with her for three months. Then after that, I was on the road with Clarence Henry.

She [Billie Holiday] was a hell of a person. All I know was she would get onstage and charm the shit out you. Excuse my language. Ben Webster was on the gig. We had a hell of a time, me and the other saxophone, Andy Williams, waiting on Ben to come up and do something, to play. But Billie was always herself. She had that little thing about her. The first time I heard her do "Strange Fruit"—I got chills when she said, "Black bodies on the poplar trees."

I remember driving into New York, and Leo [Luche, the bassist] said, "Wake up, there's the Statue of Liberty."

I looked up there and saw it and said, "Yeah, I'll be back." That was a hell of a feeling because you'd always see it from the movies. People coming in on the boats and being liberated. I came to New York and stuck to it like glue.

In between, I was playing gigs with Sun Ra. I been here ever since.

Bill Banfield: Tell me about the formation of the Retinue band with Pat.

Charles Davis: We just came up with the idea. It wasn't preplanned. We fell into it and we did it. I wrote an arrangement on Cherokee. Pat had "Little Niecey." [He sings it.] We had different arrangements. Charles Greenly. He wrote "El Seno," a Cecil Payne arrangement of Flying Fish. We made a few little gigs, a TV show [with Amiri Baraka], made it up to Hartford at the park up there. We got a grant over there for something at the jazz cultural theater. We had a few gigs.

Bill Banfield: What were your discussions and interactions like?

Charles Davis: We got a gig over here, a gig over there. It wasn't like the modern jazz quartet. We were scuffling to get it together. We were all struggling then. But Pat Patrick was a hell of a musician, composer, creator. I remember in the Chicago days, there was a hit of his they used to play on the jukebox; it was called "Down Pat" on Argo records, I believe. It was a D♭ flat blues. This was in the 1950s.

He was dedicated. I remember when he was sick. We were there at a party for Clifford Jordan back in Chicago. Pat was living with this bassist then, Ernest Outlaw. He was sick then. I was there, and I saw him. He and Outlaw played together with James Moody. It was the summer. I said to him, "Where you staying?" He said, "I'm living with Ernest." They shared an apartment.

Bill Banfield: It's something to be a dedicated musician, just dedicated to that music; nothing like it?

Charles Davis: That's true. Between you and the creator. You take care of the music, and the creator will take care of you.

Bill Banfield: Wise and wonderfully put. We thank you for this.

RICHARD EVANS

We had the chance to interview another member of Sun Ra's band, Richard Evans. We spent time together on April 23, 2013. Richard Evans, who describes himself as having taken "some lessons" from Pat Patrick and Sun Ra, arranged and produced platinum gold hits and some of the biggest and most memorable Natalie Cole recordings a decade later in the 1970s. These included "This Will Be," "Our Love," "Everlasting Love," "Unforgettable You," "I Got Love on My Mind," "Inseparable," and many more. The Chicago connections among band teacher Dyett, Nat King Cole, Pat Patrick, Sun Ra, Richard Evans, and Natalie Cole are notable. Evans taught arranging at Berklee College of Music for twenty-five years. This was the last time we spoke. Richard Evans passed in 2014.

Bill Banfield: Tell me a little bit about your relationship with Pat Patrick.

Richard Evans: Pat gave me a few hints about arranging. I stole a lot of things from watching him. The most impressive thing was that he was a very handsome dude who was very kind, a sweet-hearted kind of guy. Everyone liked him. He was very friendly, a very positive kind of guy, and Pat was very apt and astute.

Bill Banfield: How did you connect with Sun Ra?

Richard Evans: I met Sun Ra in August 1955. I was just out the army and joined his band in September. I learned from him that everything did not have to have a chord. I learned independent line writing from Sun Ra.

Pat Patrick was in the band then, and he was a beautiful cat. I left by November but returned later to record *Space Is the Place.* Sun Ra was was talking about being from Saturn! From Saturn? I'm from Birmingham, where he's from, and I ain't never seen no Saturn, Alabama!

Sun Ra was always into people's business, starting fires and smoke bombs. Guys were afraid of him. He told [John] Gilmore, "John, did you do that arrangement yet?" I was there, and John said, "No, but I can do it tomorrow." Sun Ra said, "Look here, do it, or your mother is going to jail."

After so many times, I got out of there. I made a poster for him one time. I was studying art. It was a great poster, so I brought it to him one day. He laughed, and they all said, "We don't play jazz, we play dazz." So I quit. I couldn't deal with all that stuff, fraternity and all that. I went to church and I had a dominating father already.

Pat was playing alto at that time. Sun Ra would write, and he had Pat, Julian Priester, John Gilmore, and Dave Young on trumpet. Sometimes, Pat played baritone.

Sun Ra wrote horn parts, and he sounded like Ellington. He wouldn't write anything for the bass. That would leave the bass all alone. He didn't have a chord chart for the bass player.

Another thing he'd do is have me playing on upright, then another guy playing electric bass!

He really didn't understand acoustics. He did a lot of experimenting with things that didn't work.

Pat, he was a damn good arranger. I stole from him. The thing I learned from him was to be nice to people.

I was playing bass in 1962 and I moved into my own apartment and Paul Winter called me up for some arrangements. John Hammond had signed him.

After some rehearsals and seeing they liked my arrangements and playing, they invited me to tour. We left out on our way to South America, Haiti, Central America, Chile, Argentina, Brazil, then we returned July 1962. Then in September 1962, I was playing with Amad Jamal, right in the middle of the Cuban Missile Crisis. I stayed with him from 1962 to 1964. I went on to write for Ramsey Lewis in 1964 and 1965. That was my first big smash. I did an arrangement of "Have Yourself a Soulful Little Christmas" for Kenny Burrell, and "Ode to 52nd Street." From these, we had "Soul-ero," that was a smash for him. I was the head arranger at Cadet Records from 1964 to 1967.

I did all those hits arrangements for Cadet Records, *The Soulful Strings*, those were called, *Paint It Black*, all out of Chicago. Then I went to be head producer and A&R director at Chess Records from 1967 to 1970. Then I worked with Natalie Cole, from about December 1974 through 1980, but that's a whole other story.

PAT PATRICK INTERVIEW

This interview with Pat Patrick was conducted by Phil Schaap, on his show celebrating the Thelonious Monk Festival, aired on March 16, 1976, on WKCR, 89.9. Patrick provides fantastic insight into the band workings of Monk and Duke Ellington. The interview reveals how much Patrick cares about the two icons, about the music in general, and about the state of African American music traditions. Pat Patrick beautifully articulates what he understands traditions, discipline, and great musicianship to be, as well as what makes Monk and Ellington distinctive and of note. It is also interesting that Pat linked the two icons because he had toured with both of them and could speak from personal experience. We hear the clarity of his ideas and his eloquence, sensitivity, and humor as he explains what true, deep musicianship means and how great musicianship can be measured.

Pat Patrick: I guess a lot depends on who knows you or who you know in the business. At this time, Wilbur Ware was playing with Thelonious Monk. I think they had played one weekend or so prior to the time that I came into the group. I think they had even played one or two nights of that week already, when, rather abruptly, Charley Rouse left the group. So they needed someone right away to come in and finish out the week. I was living around the corner from Wilbur Ware, and I assumed that they hadn't been able to find anyone available at the time. But anyway, Monk had given everyone notice to see who they could come up with. Wilbur knew me. He and I had played together a lot in Chicago. He came by the house one afternoon and asked me if I wanted to make the gig down there. I figured I'd come down and play my baritone, that would be nice. But I thought the group had been with tenor saxophone for so long. So anyway we discussed that, and they said, "Come on down."

I had all kinds of apprehension about it because I didn't really know what to do, whether to take the baritone, the tenor, or what. I knew one thing about it that made me leery was the fact that, although I've listened to Monk for a long time and knew some of his music, it was all on the E♭ instrument, and I knew the problems I'd be confronted with trying to transpose those things instantaneously on the spot. Particularly with the maestro himself, you see, so . . .

But I guess just the plain desire to play with him got the better of my better judgment. And so I went down there, you know, and I didn't really expect to last more than the night or, if that long, a couple of sets. I really did it out of the sheer desire to play with him at least once.

This was one of the very high points in my musical career. For him to—after the first night—ask me was I going to be back tomorrow night to finish out the week, when I never had any idea that I would be there any longer than the one night, that was big.

I didn't feel that I brought anything special to his music or anything like that. I just figured I was just there to fill out until they got who they were looking for, or wanted to "make the gig." So for him the ask me back, that really flipped me out. I'll never forget that. This is one of the greatest compliments I've ever gotten. [Before Patrick, there had been Charley Rouse, Coleman Hawkins, Sonny Rollins, and John Coltrane.]

I can be very grateful to the man in his consideration of me, because he steered clear of his more difficult music, I think, for the first few days or weeks that I played with him. He kind of stayed close to the things he felt I could handle. A couple of times he would play something that I really didn't think I could deal with in the melodic line. So I would lay out and he would play it, and I would just come in on the bridge or something and make it through that way until I had a chance to brush up on some of these things around the house. I had never really gone into any depth playing his music, because I had always played the alto primarily, because when I started listening to Bird and guys like that, I was playing the alto. Everything I tried to play was from the alto. Then I switched later to the baritone when the alto was stolen.

That was the only way I could stay in the school band. Because the band instructor, Captain Walter Dyett, at Dusable High School that I was going to, was quite a strict disciplinarian. He didn't have time for you if you didn't have your equipment. He would translate that to mean that you weren't interested in the classes, and you were taking up valuable space around there and his time.

Fortunately for me, when my alto was stolen, there was a baritone saxophone in the closet that wasn't being used, one of those "old jobs." So I said, "Give me that, anything as long as I can stay in the band." I got hooked on the thing, you know. It's really a fantastic instrument. Then I ran into a guy who had one for sale that I got a hold of, and that got me started on the baritone. I guess the major portion of my learning experience happened in Chicago. Because at the time, the Regal Theater was open and they brought in shows on a weekly basis. And quite often they traveled with smaller groups, and when they got to town they would augment the nucleus they were carrying with other musicians to fill out and make a larger band. By playing on baritone saxophone, I got called in for quite a few of those things. So I had the very distinct pleasure of playing with people like Nat Cole, Don Redman, Illinois Jacket, Cootie Williams, Pearl Bailey, Eartha Kitt, Sammy Davis Jr., Redd Foxx, Flip Wilson; any number of dynamite people. Not to mention the people who were still in Chicago at the time like King Collax, Gene Ammonds, John Griffin, all those giants around town. Lots of those people were playing in clubs that if you went by there, they'd quite often let you sit in. Chicago at that time was on the ebb of one of the greatest musical episodes in the history of African American music that there has probably ever been.

I'll tell you another thing. There was a guy there that used to play with Louie Armstrong and the Earl Hines band. His name was Zilner Randolph. Recently, in New York, I ran across a reissue of some recordings, and I saw his name on them. He had a son and a daughter that played with Sun Ra at one time.

The girl sang and has recorded, and the fella played trumpet and recorded. His name is Luscious. He played very good, good musicians. He had several children and taught them all music. And if I'm not mistaken, he's still teaching out of his home. A beautiful guy. Some of the stories he used to tell me about how sometimes, without knowing, Louie would say, "You got this next solo," right at the time when it was time to blow.

And he'd have to come on like Louie Armstrong! I assumed he was able to hold the chair down simply because he was sufficient enough in his playing to be able to back Louie up. And at that time, Louie was at his greatest. Some of the stories he would tell me were fantastic, so naturally when I came across this record, I got me one and I got him a copy and took it home for him the next time I went home to Chicago.

I had worked with James Moody in one of the Regal situations. I recorded ["The Last Train from Overbrook," on Cadet] with him in Chicago, and after that he talked to me about performing in his small group, four horns and three rhythm. So I said, "Yeah, I'd love to." Eddie Jefferson was with him at the time. I think Johnny Coles, Tom Macintosh, myself, Gene Keys, a bass player, Ernest Outlaw from Chicago, and a drummer named Clarence Johnston.

And so we started working in New York in 1960. And I worked with him for about nine months.

I had seen Monk previously when he had come through Chicago on various occasions. When any of them—Bird, Prez, any of those guys—came to town, I was there! I naturally had developed an appreciation for his music, and then when I came to New York, we played a couple of times at the Apollo. Monk was there. Miles's group was there. Blakey was there. One thing that always fascinated me about Monk was his humor in his music.

Not only while he was playing, but while he wasn't even playing. At that time he would do quite a bit of dancing. When he finished his solo, he'd move out and go into his thing. And he has a very unique dance. So I saw him then a few times after that.

I can recall those first nights at the Vanguard [in New York] were nice. Then we went to Toronto at a club called the Colonial Tavern. That was in February, and we played a week there. I happened to have one of the napkins of the people who was booked in the club. And they spelled his name "The Lonius Monk Quartet"! Later in February, the 23rd or 25th, we did the jazz workshop in Boston.

Utmost in my mind is how educational this was for me to be associated with him during that period. I remember going by his house after a few weeks. I tried to encourage him to have rehearsals so I could come by and tackle some of the more difficult music. He said, "Sure, OK." And there were several attempts at this before we even sat down at the piano. He was into various things. There was a bar in the neighborhood where he used to live. He'd like to go by there and talk and rap. One time, in particular, we were fooling around at his piano. It's his harmonic concept, and the unusual manner in which he hears intervals. This coupled with his personality, which has quite a bit of humor. If you listen to all the great musicians that I know of, there are distinct qualities of humor in their playing. I think this sets him apart. I tend to think you can hear his music much easier than you can play it. Because some of the things I even figured were relatively easy, posed quite a bit of difficulty. The way he comps [accompanies] behind you, it's sort of like a guiding light. If you can open up your ears, mind, and tune in on it, he'll show you the way to go. You know right away when you are outside of what he's doing, if that's hardly to be imagined that you could play outside of Monk's music, but I suppose it can happen accidentally from time to time. [He laughs.]

One of the guys that I feel is doing that well is Sonny Rollins. He did a magnificent job of playing his music. Coleman Hawkins, Johnny Griffin, John Coltrane, all brought their own personalities to the music, and it grew to be something else. He would say so many things that would crack you up on the bandstand. "Hey, man, Wilbur must have a gun on me. He doesn't want me to play. He must have a gun." That gives you an idea of where his humor was.

I had another very distinct musical experience: to have had the opportunity to play with one of Monk's influences, and that's Duke Ellington. And that happened in a very chance way. It just so happens that I knew the road manager who knew me from Chicago. And so at the time they were going on a road tour for a week, Russell Procope, he decided he needed to take off for that week, and they needed a replacement. At the time, I didn't even have my own alto.

Duke has been one of my major influences all along my entire life. I remember when I first started playing anything, my father was a trumpet player, and he used to have all these Duke records around the house. I used to listen to them before I went to school. Sometimes I'd get halfway to school and think about a record I had just heard and I'd turn around and go listen to it again. So I said yes to Duke, grabbed instruments I had borrowed, and jumped on the bus.

When we got to the first stop in West Virginia, Paul Gonsalves and Harry Carney took me to the side and showed me the book and some tunes we might be going over. The music is mountainous, of course.

I was eager to get on that bandstand with the band. That week with Duke, I can't describe the impact on me, finding yourself thrust in the midst of all that music, sitting on one side, Harry Carney, and on the other side, Johnny Hodges. It was five one-nighters that we did on the road throughout Ohio.

It was a magnificent experience. I remember one night, Ray Nance played something that was so beautiful and powerful. It is hard to imagine. What a dynamic musician he was. Of course Duke himself, he did some very phenomenal things.

For instance, I was playing one arrangement, and at the end of this arrangement, he would cue the brass, reeds, trombones, as a final chord on the end of a song.

I was constantly trying to catch up with what's going on, so the next night that we played this particular arrangement, I said, "Well, I'm going to be on my toes and be ready so I won't have my head buried in the music. I'll look up and be professional and everything." And so I looked ahead and got my note together, and so I'm waiting on the maestro to give the saxophones the chord, and I hit it nice and strong and everything, and I noticed Duke kind of flinched a little bit, and he looked over my way and then he gave the rest of the chords and took it out. And so I said, "I wonder what was wrong?" I looked back at the paper and saw I played the right note, but I played an octave too low. And he heard it. [He laughs.] That reed section was phenomenal at that time. Johnny Hodges, Harry Carney, Jimmy Hamilton, Paul Gonsalves. In that entire band the musicians' own musicianship became a part of what Duke Ellington, the maestro, drew from. I would think that I've been very fortunate to have played with the likes of Sun Ra, Monk, and Duke. A lifetime of learning right there.

Writings of Pat Patrick, Matter, Notes

$\mathcal{O}$ne of the most revealing parts of the Pat Patrick collection is the huge voice we hear in his writings. His is the voice of a musician with ideas beyond playing music. It's as if music is the sounding board, the first conversation that initiates a broader dialogue. That's what you feel in his writing: that there is a deep wisdom in these musical traditions and that the musicians are the soldiers carrying the lines of that deeper truth. Pat Patrick takes this gift seriously.

And from these writings, we share here important excerpts, including a short but potent article from which we have frequently quoted. It is entitled "Our Music: Yesterdays, Todays and Tomorrows," and was published as part of *Black Theatre Magazine* in 1976. We print it here in its entirety.

Pat Patrick also kept notes. He had notes on arrangements, notes about family genealogies, notes on other notes about notes on which he wrote notes. And of course there were musical notes, scores on which he too wrote notes. We talked about larger themes and nuggets of truth. The notes selected here are gems of truth about significant points Patrick wanted to make. These come out in his letters, articles, radio shows, or in his music. Pat Patrick was a thinker, and he wrote down many of his ideas.

Of course his ideas were an important extension of the context of the times in which he was making music, and much of his thinking focuses on Black music and musicianship. Additionally, the sociocultural aesthetic at the time, for Patrick, was Black nationalism and race pride, and at the heart of that was the concern for the preservation of Black heritage, especially in music. This is also clear in Patrick's writing.

Amiri Baraka provided us very early on with the book's golden axis of meaning here. Although these issues may seem distant today, they are always at the core of Black musicians' thoughts, largely due to how music culture is set up. That "setup"—to make money in a capitalist society—is always tricky when discussing art. You have to have musicians to make the music. The music has to be produced, packaged, distributed, and marketed. We are often unaware of that longer chain of delivery.

But in these discussions, the musicians are always the ones who feel the delight and the dangers in this process, and many times, are on the short end of receiving monetary benefits and proper credit and recognition, especially Black musicians. To read Pat Patrick's concerns on this topic is to read generations of musicians who addressed this rather fiercely, from Scott Joplin to James Reese Europe to Louis Armstrong to Miles Davis to Pat Patrick to Prince.

Pat Patrick's generation was a group who demanded to be recognized in the literal sense of documenting Black people as leaders of ideas. And so he—like many of the vocal individuals from this period such as Malcolm X, Gwendolyn Brooks, or Amiri Baraka—traces his dedication to W. E. B. Du Bois and the "race men and women" from earlier eras who advocated for the "Black voice."

This advocacy as represented and evidenced by Pat Patrick has always been a part of Black artistry. Upward mobility as a search for the face of dignity meant cultural achievement, and with cultural achievement came empowerment, equality, and agency, which included the tools to critique and challenge the status quo. These ideas fueled the 1960s and 1970s and were deeply important to Patrick.

By the time he began performing, musicians had created an enormous range of American expressions, and yet many still felt locked into the chains of restricted expression as this relates to mass exposure, media coverage, and industry distribution of their products, oftentimes most visibly seen in the commercial marketplaces. Certainly in the 1960s and 1970s, there still were not enough Black executives or industry captains present or given positions of power.

Pat Patrick fits squarely in the middle of the Black arts movement. That movement was an extremely powerful and critically important impulse in African American arts expression that focused on moving Black people to establish their own publishing houses, magazines, journals, art institutions, community music, and arts movements. The major Black arts literary publication was the short-lived (1969–1972) *Black Theatre Magazine*. This was the literary vehicle in which Pat Patrick began to record his thoughts. We hope you find these excerpts as powerful as we have.

OUR MUSIC: YESTERDAYS, TODAYS AND TOMORROWS BY PAT PATRICK, 1973

Herein are a few thoughts about our musical art form, which I have been involved with most of my so-called life, that I hope will clear away some of the fog of misconception surrounding the same. Having walked it, talked it, ate it, slept it, wept it and kept it, for the better part of thirty years, mostly as a scuffling, Black musician on a "so-called" professional level in this economic-orientated society, I can testify to how messed up the music scene is if nothing else. How I relate what I've seen and experienced will be for real if not always understood. Fortunately those things learned by trial and error have afforded me a better insight with less frustration about what I see happening in the world with regards to Black music.

I suppose that it would appear to a lot of young people that the world/ life of a musician, particularly a rock, pop musician these days is a very glamorous and lucrative life to get into. This may be often true for a white person (with no talent) than for a Black musician with all kinds of abilities to play. Therefore, my statements are directed towards the naive, the confused and frustrated among the young, gifted and Black musicians inclined who might be thinking of or already pursuing a career in music. In America and in Europe from what I have seen, it is the same game going down. "Sure, play your music and we'll even come to see you once or twice, but don't expect a payment comparable to your efforts." First of all keep in mind (and it has been proven) that the world finds value in and wants our music. And though there is often a cold hostile reaction towards us, our music and culture in general, there is still a need for it. Can you dig it?

When after the world exhausts all means to try to learn how to assimilate jazz, they in turn promote it as jazz, which it is, but as jazz is not authentic. What the Afro-American plays is jazz because he has lived it. It is a part of his heritage. Therein lies the difference, and that is the story of what has been happening to our music to this very day. So what is the reason that it is being claimed as their own by some of these assimilations of jazz? Simple: It has proven to be a highly commercial product. The original sounds that have had so much to do with the foundation and the formation of our culture has through the ages been used and misused for all sorts of purposes other than what the music was/is intended for. Seems that the music often heard these days no matter how one thinks he enjoys it (it too often reflects sex and or lovemaking) is not contributing enough towards a greater awareness for Black folks. Perhaps the world would not be in a chaotic state if natural orders of laws had been followed. This is not to say that notable or worthy music has not come along in the past. But too often, as in the case of the Black man, many benefits derived from his work have been diverted away from him and his people by something or other. This is no accident but rather a carefully worked out conspiracy. Music is a high medium of art. There can be no disputing the rapid communicative properties of music and its ability to reach all people. Therefore, high standards should be maintained by its practitioners and high values by its adherents if music is to weave its magic spell. Everyone comes in contact, involved with, or influenced by music at some point in their lives. Everybody hums a tune sometime in their life even when not particularly thinking about music, so great is its effect upon the subconscious mind. Music is a natural phenomenon that can lift a person out of the doldrums of this world and its problems.

Can you imagine life here if there were no music at all?

Yet we need to be aware of what I call "contrived music." That which has been carefully studied and arranged to have certain desired effects on folks. Now, loudness and energetic showmanship does not always mean that meaningful music is being played. All music is not truly inspired. It varies in degrees of artistry. Too long it has been used to propagate other things besides music, like music to sell cars by, cigarettes by, this by, that by, etc. Consequently, seeing what has happened in the past, know for sure that what is happening now will have its effect on the future. Therefore a concerned effort should be made, particularly by the Black musicians, to improve on his music's quality and not allow that quality to be cut, watered down or misused.

Now, all music, if it's going to mean very much, should have a message, tell a story and surely some do, but also let the message therein could be detrimental to the listener.

Since so many of our messengers (light bearers) have left here, some it would seem prematurely; with the accent on volume and repetition, much of the real message has been lost entirely or become distorted leaving much to be desired. People have been conditioned to accepting mediocrity. A classic example is oleomargarine. Now, it looks like butter, it tastes something like it, but it's not. Of course if you eat it long enough you might develop a taste for it and if you were raised on it you may not like the real butter at all. Furthermore, with everybody playing the same kind of instruments through the same kind of amplifiers and speakers, their own identity tends to get squashed leaving everybody sounding alike, unless you are very creative.

So in looking at our music with regards to its content, its message, yesterdays and todays, I would say that the music was happier in earlier times and has become steadily more gloomy and sad down to the present. If this is to be considered a trend, then we can only imagine that it will get worse as we move towards the future. This type of movement in an art form is not progress and is unnatural. Of course there is cause and effect but what will be done about it?

To improve on this situation is a monumental task that only true art and artists can accomplish. Simple music tends to keep its listeners simple. At this time there is a definite need for Black people to know and understand, appreciate their own culture, to be able to recognize, desire it and not be ashamed of it in this environment we live, exist in, lest our own unique identity dwindle and disappear. We must be aware that our hearing is not dulled by the drone of meaningless music. With all this you might raise the question: Where is real music? Where can it be found and how does it sound? I would offer as a suggestion to try the Sun Ra Arkestra. And how do you distinguish real music from jive music? Real is that which is inspiring, spontaneous and stimulating. Jive is that which is monotonously repetitious.

Our job here should be to try to help in rebuilding a people's culture that has been prostrated, raped for centuries, and yet is in this so-called space age, still a major source of ideas and inspiration. Proving to all of reasonable mentality that it is of real value, not just to the people through whom it has come, but to the world. It is also possible that any ideas absorbed here by the reader and maybe even adhered to can at best have a small effect on what's happening now.

However, it is with greater concern that we address ourselves to the future (our children), with whom in time and on time we exchange positions. May I add at this point that whether you agree or disagree, the fact is that the reason this world is messed up is because of its musical disarrangement. It's out of tune with nature.

EXCERPTS FROM PATRICK'S NOTES

These are literally just little notes Patrick wrote to himself, written on dozens and dozens of little individual scraps of paper, on the backs of envelopes, on the backsides of flyers, or on manuscript paper. Notes and ideas for us are seen here as inextricably bound and provide evidence that music was likened to social, artistic, and political ideas for Patrick.

"It took the so-called revolutionary atmosphere just for me to be able to play for my folks again. That to me is progress."

"What America, particularly the younger set, is just beginning to understand and appreciate, what the rest of the world has been aware of to a greater degree, is the universality of Black Afro-American music."

"Many people are saying many things, for instance, white musicians who have just learned how to play a little jazz, and yet are so open in putting down jazz musicians and Black musicians in general. You don't expect someone to knock what they themselves are doing, especially if they are making money at it. I say, 'Fuck what they say.' Would you deny a dying man his last rights in terms of saying whatever he wants to say in his effort to save himself?"

"We should begin to pay more attention to our common sayings and street sayings and from where and how it comes into being. Such as, 'Black poems,' 'Right on,' and the much popularized hand slap that's been a tradition among Black men for a long time, and what we see on the football, basketball and other sports fields. These days, they like other things of our heritage are constantly being used and exploited by no less 'the big commercial enterprises' to push and sell their products on TV, radio, etc. And why? Because 'our thing' gives 'their thing' that human quality that makes them attractive to the prospective buyer."

To his editor, Patrick wrote, "Hook this in with the beat article. This column is open for suggestions, inquiries and any letters dealing with Black music from a folklore, historical or contemporary point of view. With the idea in mind that this should become a healthy avenue for exchange of ideas and information."

"To find out how to cripple and destroy the system, find out where it gets its fuel and power, just as fire must have oxygen to burn. . . . Do a play on 'the philosophy in Black Blues singers.' Prepare for your seed sown."

"I've got the right to sing the Blues. . . . I've got a line for you. All them, from Jesus, Mohammed, Ramses, Moses on down died, and left me here to deal with this bullshit by myself, and I don't see any help from them. . . . If they were dealing with ordinary people like the people or the system of the day, they should have done better according to my way of seeing it."

"How all ofays [white Americans] have a Black edifice in their home to train their attack dogs on. Darkies need to stop repeating the idle phrases that come into fad. Where are all the people who say they believe in the Bible, and what about the part that says, 'No, in the days when they say, peace. . . ?' To the silent minority: the Bible tells Egypt to be silent. All those who are being Black have learned the art of survival in this insane sadistic Western society."

"Memory Measures Intellect: If Niggers forget how to swing, no matter what they are doing, they might as well be white all the way. . . . The new system, 'value system' for Blacks and all people."

"The system today is basically the same system that was instituted when this country was founded. Slavery was a part of that system's makeup because it was found to be profitable. That same system functions the same ways and people are involved in it when knowingly or not, because of its monetary profits and economic gains. It is as much American as apple pie or hot dogs. And the masses of people exist according to their positions in it."

ON EDUCATION

The following excerpt was an unfinished installment of Patrick's music articles for *Black Theatre Magazine*. It was taken from draft notes for the next article to be published, date unknown. It was written to address Pat's own interest in education and focused on two prominent examples of fine educators that he knew firsthand, Captain Walter Dyett and Dr. William P. Foster. Both of these men he admired deeply. William P. Foster was hired to rebuild Florida A&M University's marching band program in 1946. Foster built what was called "Marching 100," to be one the nation's best marching bands, and it became internationally famous. By the time of this correspondence, the Florida A&M band number was at 196, an all-male marching band that NBC and *Life* magazine had called the number-one marching band in the country and the greatest halftime show in America. Foster's work and his band had been featured in *Time* magazine and *Ebony* and reviewed by papers across the United States. It was featured at the 1963 Orange Bowl game that aired on CBS and appeared during an NFL game in Cleveland Stadium in 1964.

Patrick, here, is engaging another strata of the music industry: college educators, and in this case, marching band directors within the academy. This connects him again not only to Captain Walter Dyett but to Sun Ra, who aspired to be a music educator as well. Pat Patrick is focused on the benefits of music education to sharpen concentration skills, molding the minds of our young to help them strive toward artistic expression and equipping them for success in the future.

Patrick writes in his unfinished draft,

> Be assured in mind that if any of these ideas are considered by the reader and perhaps reacted upon, it can at best have a small effect upon today. It is therefore with greater interest that we address ourselves to the future, our children, whom in time we exchange positions.
>
> In music as in everything else, a person desires to do and do well, basic training is very important. Of course the type of basic training can differ

and the types of practitioners produced will vary. But if in the main, they strive towards the artistic expression, this in itself will speak of the type of basic training that was adhered to. Then, too, this gets to be another issue and problem when the masses get to the point where they can't distinguish between art and junk. Too often we are exposed to more junk than more art and consequently our tastes begin to adhere to more junk. This comes from a lack of exposure to the real thing. Then you can see where those who have never been exposed to real music will be coming from. This is called false or "jive indoctrination."

So at this time I would like to focus on a few of those who have played an important part in molding the minds of our young. Those who did so much to instill in the youth the quality of dedicated concentration. This is so important for anything that a person tries to do and expects to do well. Many times when we see our children unable or unwilling to sit still and be attentive and listen when in class or an assembly or other group gatherings where there is something to be learned, it is because their powers of concentration have been destroyed. This is the type of power we as Black people should be most concerned with.

At this date in time, because today's youth is definitely the future generation, they must be equipped if they expect to survive under the advanced pressure.

One such organizer in the arts that we have who's been doing a tremendous job over the years is the chairman of the music department at Florida A&M University, Dr. William P. Foster.

Here is a person who, as the result of his sprit, dedication to the high ideals and standards, has built an institution in music and the marching band category in particular.

Having graduated from high school, I received a scholarship to go to FAMU. Along with Dr. Foster, one who has to be among the greatest to come along, Captain Walter Dyett, who has had a very impressive number of fine musicians to graduate from his bands. A man who remained at his post giving of himself to all those who came through his portals. Even after failing health had crippled him. Although I was unable at the time to follow through on the scholarship, many of my school buddies went to FAMU and some stayed.

To become music teachers. . . . [Uncompleted from his handwritten draft.]

The following letter from Dr. William P. Foster, dated January 18, 1972, indicates the above article was to be published. Dr. Foster here was congratulating Pat Patrick on his appointment as music news editor of *Black Theatre Magazine.*

College of Arts and Sciences
Mr. Pat Patrick
2349 Seventh Avenue
New York, New York 100300
January 18, 1972

Dear Mr. Patrick:

This communication comes to acknowledge and to express appreciation for your letter of January 12, 1972, newspaper article and literature on Black Theater, I was particularly impressed with the Black Theater material. I wish to express commendations and felicitations for your achievements and attainments as music editor of the *Black Theatre Magazine*. In regards to your request for soulful band members, I am asking our arrangers to consider releasing several of the arrangements made for the FAMU Marching Band to send to Salah Ragob in Egypt. As soon as an answer is received from our arrangers, I will inform you of the decision regarding release of arrangements. I look back with pleasant memories on the days of Captain Walter Dyett and the many outstanding musicians he sent to Florida A and M.

In regards to your future article in the *Black Theatre Magazine*, enclosed find my vita and literature on the FAMU Band.

Best wishes and kindest personal regards.

Sincerely
William P. Foster
Chairman
Department of Music

· *11* ·

Last Days
Interview with Pat Patrick's Sister, Sheila Miles

$\mathcal{A}$fter a health incident while visiting with his children Deval and Rhonda in Boston, Pat decided to return to Chicago for a potentially more profitable gig scene sometime in 1990. The concern about his health and a need for more work brought him home, back to his roots in the Midwest. During this time his sister, Sheila Miles, recalls his hip was bothering him and that he was not doing so well, all around.

There were gigs on the north side of Chicago, and Charles Davis affirmed as well that he was probably living with his old friend Earnest Outlaw. He had a cemented group with a singer, and he began to have some steady work, but he became even more ill. He then decided to move to East Moline to be with his family. That time in his family home was to be less than three months before his passing. On November 3, 1991, shortly before he died, his friends held a benefit concert for him in Chicago to raise money for his medical expenses. The flyer read,

> For Jazz Lovers: A Benefit for a Local Jazzman Pat Patrick, Sunday, November 3, 1991, Time: 3PM until 7 PM, Place: Ancient Egyptian Museum, Chicago, IL 60653. Some of Chicago's Great Musicians will be performing. Donations can be sent to the Ancient Egyptian Museum, payable to Laurdine "Pat" Patrick; Goal: To pay off bills before relocating to Moline, IL Celebration: Please join us to celebrate our association with Pat for the past 45 years or so, and to express our friendship and love. Contribution: $20; Free Food, Live Music.

To the very end, he was a respected, revered, and cared-for musician, and he was still performing.

" FOR JAZZ LOVERS "

A BENEFIT FOR A
LOCAL JAZZMAN PAT PATRICK

DATE: SUNDAY, NOVEMBER 3, 1991

TIME: 3 P.M. UNTIL 7 P.M.

PLACE: ANCIENT EGYPTIAN MUSEUM
3849 So. MICHIGAN
CHICAGO, IL. 60653

SOME OUR CHICAGO'S GREAT MUSICIANS WILL
BE PERFORMING.* DONATION $20.00/xx

* DONATIONS CAN BE SENT TO THE ANCIENT EGYPTIAN
MUSEUM, PAYABLE LAURDINE "PAT" PATRICK.

BENEFIT & CELEBRATION FOR PAT PATRICK
Benefit: Just released from hospital-Must convalesce
for indefinite period.
Goal: To pay off bills before relocating to
Moline, Ill.
Celebration: Please join us to celebrate our
association with Pat for the past 45 years or so,
and to express our friendship and love.

DATE: Sunday, Nov. 3, 1991   3 P.M. Until 7 P.M.
Place: Ancient Egyptian Museum
3849 S. Michigan - Chicago, Il. 60653
Contribution: $20.00 - If You can't attend please
send contribution to: Laurdine "Pat" Patrick
%Ancient Egyptian Museum - 3849 S. Michigan-Chgo.
For INfo Call: Walter at 268 3700 / Paul 241-6885
    FREE FOOD   LIVE - MUSIC
    SPREAD THE WORD   --   CALL A FRIEND

Benefit Flyer
From the Pat Patrick Archive

INTERVIEW WITH PAT PATRICK'S
SISTER, SHEILA MILES

In May 2014, we had the opportunity to interview Pat's sister, Sheila Miles. Sheila helped us to see the kind of man Pat was from childhood until the end of his life.

Bill Banfield: Sheila, tell me about Pat—what kind of person he was, his personality, and what you remember during those difficult years between Chicago and New York in the 1960s.

Sheila Miles: My brother was a sweet person. I remember the years I was growing up, around the same time as my nieces and nephew in Chicago. My brother in the early 1960s would play at the Regal Theater, and we would get in for free to see him. This was when he was traveling back and forth. La'Shon's mom was a beautiful woman, but she was sick. So her aunt raised La'Shon.

And at that time, parents and grandparents used to hide things and not let the children know. My mom used to take me over there, and my mom was coming over there to see La'Shon quite a bit. I was happy that happened. I never wanted La'Shon to be left out.

I think Pat figured the opportunities would be better for him in New York. He felt there was a much larger span, a variety of music that he wanted to get into. My brother was a unique player. His sound was very unique on the baritone horn.

That big horn. He carried that great big horn and he was not a big person. He was small. He just felt that things would be better for him working in New York. At this time in Chicago, it was hard for the Black players with the unions. They wouldn't hire the musicians. So he felt it would be better for him in New York.

The complication was that he wanted to move to New York and Emily [his wife] didn't want to leave. I think he would have been much happier if he were able to have had his family there.

Emily never felt she wanted to live in New York. She didn't think that was the life, with all the "rat race." She felt better and safe with the kids being in Chicago with her mom. She put Deval through school.

I've seen the letters back and forth. There were times, I'm sure, Deval was upset at his dad. My brother was very opinionated, and so was Deval. There was resentment. My brother had been all over the world, met a lot of people. He didn't want Deval to be manipulated by rich folks. He wanted him to be the down-to-earth type. He didn't want Deval to be thought of as an "Uncle Tom." They had lots of conflicts over that. My brother just thought he was going to be "bought off." These were the two power struggles during these times. So I can understand where they both were coming from. It's too bad that Pat could not see how all this would come down the line and mellow out. They were both strong individuals in their beliefs.

But Deval's father was always in and out of his life.

Bill Banfield: Can you shed more light on Pat Patrick's last days in East Moline where he passed? The questions surrounding his archives, how they got out of Chicago?

Sheila Miles: One of the last efforts was his Baritone Sax Retinue. That was his last working in that era in New York. He had gotten a second divorce by this time, too.

When my brother passed away, his horns were all spread in several trunks that he had. Many of the things he had were left at my mother's house. She spread out everything for Deval, Rhonda, and La'Shon to look through. They came a few days before the funeral and took a whole day going through the things left by their dad for them. He had it all organized, written up on paper.

Deval took a guitar. There was a piccolo. My mother kept a Mach 6 saxophone. And that saxophone went to Kenny G. Kenny G bought that saxophone from us. I sold it to Kenny G. We wanted a musician who was in music to have that saxophone.

At that time, Kenny G played at the arena here in East Moline. I ran into him and told him it needed pads but was a beautiful horn. I told my aunt, and my mom, they took pictures with Kenny G and the horn. He liked the tone of the saxophone. When my brother was living in Chicago, he had things to put in storage. There might have been other things among these that were in there as well. He put a lot of things in Chicago in storage.

I think the remainder of things besides what we had were left in Chicago, and those I think now were the things that ended up being shipped to Boston to Deval.[1]

During this time in Chicago in 1990, he was living on the north side and playing gigs with a group of his musician friends. My brother took real sick in the wintertime, the year he died. He died hours before the new year. He came down to East Moline in November. He was again in Chicago staying with this buddy of his in 1991.

Maybe he was there about six months or a year in Chicago before this. When he came, he had just recovered from pneumonia. He came to East Moline from Chicago. The cold was so bad, and he was very sick at this time. I had a house that my mom and I bought. He stayed right next to my mom's room. Everybody had a lot of space in the house. During this time, he was playing his music. Our uncle, my mother's brother, Covert Dixon, lived in nearby Moline as well and was very close to Pat. He died just a few years ago. Pat was a homebody, very quiet. He liked to socialize with his family.

But those days he was just listening to music and writing music. His music was his natural high. He loved his music. He knew he had leukemia, but I think the weather and his hip got to him, too. When he got to us he was very sick. He said he wasn't doing good. My mom tried to keep him out of the cold. He wrote music and letters, but we noticed he kept coughing. I looked after him. I'm a nurse. He didn't look good. We called the ambulance, and the ambulance took him to Moline Heights Hospital. On the way there, a block before they got to the hospital, the ambulance got into an accident! That was weird. But they got him there. The doctors were shocked because he looked so good.

Pat asked us specifically that if he were close to death, he did not want any resuscitation if anything were to happen to him during the time he was there. He was writing music at the hospital.

The doctor couldn't believe how young he looked. My mom and my brother both looked very young. But his insides were sickly. He looked like was he was in his forties. My brother stayed in the hospital not quite a month.

He went into the hospital near the end of November . . . maybe it was three weeks before he passed. My mother, her brother, a cousin, and I were at the hospital. We were all with him. He had a recording machine [cassette player] that was right there by his bed that he was listening to. . . . My son is into music because of his Uncle Pat. He listens to Pat's music and produces beats to it.

We were all there with him when he took his last breaths. His mom was the one who shut his eyes closed. It was a beautiful thing. He was peaceful about all this. He embraced his death. I was glad to see this.

My mother told him in those last hours that he was going to be "one of those heavenly great musicians who played all the music in heaven." And Pat just chuckled.

November 23, 1929   December 31, 1991

MEMORIAL SERVICE

FOR LAURDINE "PAT" PATRICK

MONDAY, JANUARY 20, 1992
11:00 A.M.

GAINES CHAPEL A.M.E. CHURCH
311 - 19TH STREET
EAST MOLINE, IL

REV. CHARLES B. JACKSON, OFFICIATING

MR. LESTER WALTON, MUSICIAN

Pat Patrick Memorial Service
From the Pat Patrick Archive

Friday, Jan. 3, 1992

'Pat' Patrick Jr., 62

EAST MOLINE — A memorial service for Laurdine "Pat" Patrick Jr., 62, of 1418 5th Ave., will be at Gaines Chapel AME Church, East Moline, at a later date.

Mr. Patrick

The body has been cremated.

Esterdahl Mortuary Ltd., Moline, is in charge of arrangements.

Mr. Patrick died Tuesday at United Medical Center, Moline.

He was a musician and teacher and had worked with many major performing artists. His most widely recorded composition, "Yeh Yeh," was used in the movie "Good Morning Vietnam."

He married Emily Wintersmith in 1954 in Chicago.

He studied music with Capt. Walter Dyett at Chicago's DuSable High School and graduated with a music scholarship to Florida A & M University, Tallahasee. He had attended Wilson Junior College, Chicago.

He received his first musical training on trumpet from his father and Clark Terry. He switched to saxophone and was tutored privately by Willie Randall of the Earl Hines Orchestra.

He began his musical career in Chicago, performing with artists such as Muddy Waters and Red Saunders. In the 1950s, he worked with stars including Sammy Davis and Erskine Hawkins. He moved to New York in the early 1960s, and toured with the James Moody Septet and Duke Ellington Orchestra. He was musical director for Mongo Santamaria Band and the Michael Olatunji Afro-American Dance Groups. Artists he appeared with included Thelonius Monk and Patti Labelle.

His background as musician, composer and arranger placed him high in Downbeat Magazine's critics' and readers' polls in the 1970s. He was an adjunct professor at State University of New York, Old Westbury College. He continued to tour with the Sun Ra Arkestra more than 25 years, through the 1980s.

Memorials may be made to the church.

Survivors include daughters, Rhonda Seigh, San Diego, and Lashan Roberts, Chicago; a son, Deval, Boston; five grandchildren; his mother, LaVerne Williams, East Moline; his father, Laurdine Patrick Sr., Los Angeles; and sisters, Sheila Love, East Moline, and Darlene Patrick, Los Angeles.

And God Shall Wipe Away All Tears From Their Eyes; And There Shall Be No More Death, Neither Sorrow, Nor Crying, Neither Shall There Be Any More Pain; For Former Things Are Passed Away.

Revelations: 21:4

Pat Patrick Obituary
From the Pat Patrick Archive

November 23, 1929   *December 31, 1991*

Laurdine "Pat" Patrick

Prelude:

Processional:

Selection: By Friends

Invocation: Rev. James Moody

Scripture: 1 Corinthians 15:50 - 58

Selection: By Friends

Acknowledgements & Condolences: Church Clark

Obituary: (Read Silently)   Soft Music

Remarks by: Friend, Dr. Paul Sorrono
                                            Friend, Mr. Lester Walton

Remarks by Ministers:

Selection: By Friends

Word of Comfort: Pastor Jackson

                                                   Benediction:

Recessional: Soft Music

Dinner has been provided by the Gaines Chapel AME Church family and community friends an dwill be served for the bereaved family and friends immediately following the service in the lower level.

The family wishes to acknowledge all expressions of kindness shown to them during their time of sorrow.

Pat Patrick Memorial Service
From the Pat Patrick Archive

Pat Patrick Performing
From the Pat Patrick Archive

FROM THE LAST WILL AND TESTAMENT OF PAT PATRICK

To my mother should she survive me, I want you not to be sad but to be happy for me and you. I want to be cremated and wish that my ashes be scattered in the Mississippi River or in the wind. I want my mother and three children to work in cooperation in disposing of my estate and possessions. Please mother, Rhonda, Deval, and La'Shon, do not make my transition a long, drawn-out mournful ceremony. I had a fairly well life on this planet, in spite of all I had to suffer through. Although I did not achieve all that I would have liked to while I was here, I am not through and I will continue until the job is done to the Creator's satisfaction.

I hereby bequeath:

One Conn baritone saxophone to my son Deval Patrick. Son, this instrument previously belonged to the great Harry Carney of the Duke Ellington band. Please keep it in the family.

I bequeath the following instruments to my three children jointly:

Bass guitar, Guy Humphrey flute, Casio electric saxophone, Buescher baritone saxophone, Selmer tenor saxophone, Selmer alto saxophone, Buffet clarinet, Selmer clarinet, Linton clarinet, Gemeinhardt flute, Reynolds-Coloratura flute, Gemeinhardt piccolo, Italian flute, Bass clarinet (from Czechoslovakia), Buescher C melody saxophone, Spanish guitar.

I bequeath the entire collection of albums, records, cassettes, and videotapes to my children jointly. Certain of the audiocassettes have important historical information. Further, the Thelonious Monk equalized tapes are historically important.

I bequeath all of my original manuscripts, sheet music, notes, and other writings to my children jointly.

I bequeath any royalties or other monies from my publishing company, Down Pat Music Company, and monies from my writings and mechanical rights to my children jointly.

Postlude

*R*eviewing these clippings and Patrick artifacts allows us to see and better understand the importance of preserving the historical records of artistry. This is the only way to make real the work, to leave a true legacy, a map of where to go, and to teach the value of the past and its lessons and meaning.

PATRICK MATCHBOOKS

Among the interesting findings from the Pat Patrick archives is a collection of matchbooks. These matchbooks represent a sampling of the variety of places Pat Patrick moved through. His travels begin with a move into the vibrant Chicago performing scene in the 1940s and 1950s, and then to New York, living there for most of his adult life until returning to Chicago and East Moline right before his death. Along the way, he traveled the world, performing in city after city across the United States and Europe. In addition to his keen sense of the value of documentation, his more than sixty matchbooks chronicle a larger narrative of the performance and lodging patterns of working jazz musicians of this period. More specifically, the matchbooks show Pat Patrick's movement during the busiest times of his professional life. These specific kinds of travel markers represent his lodging and dining from Chicago to Cologne; the Virgin Islands; San Francisco; Portland, Oregon; and back to East Moline, Illinois. Some of the matchbooks are truly collector's items, such as one from the famed Birdland Club in New York.

What intrigues us most about the trail Patrick leaves us is that one imagines the many road trips, one-nighters, eating and resting places, and night joints for entertainment that are a part of the regular grind, part of the "gig" of working musicians.

In addition to the reflections, the writing, the teaching, the organizing of bands, sessions, and productions, the commitment to documentation, and performance excellence, these matchbooks remind us that, at the end of the day, the working musician is someone who has to carry the music from place to place to eat and to make a living. As we walk through Patrick's life, tracing the elements of his story, the matchbooks become a tool to help us connect the dots. Some great examples include:

Birdland, New York
Moulin Rouge, Chicago
Hotel Pacific, Hamburg, Germany
Takoma Station Tavern, Washington, D.C.
Park Central, Fort Worth, Texas
Jazz at Five Andy's, Chicago
Crusty Crab, San Pedro, California
Rick's Cafe American, Minneapolis, Minnesota
The Blackstone Hotel, Chicago
Novotel Lisbon, Lisbon, Portugal
Aux 4 Jeadis Café and Bar, Quebec
The Hilton Syracuse, Syracuse, New York
Le Pirate Beach Hotel, Marigot Bay, Saint Lucia
Penn Harris Inn, Camp Hill, Pennsylvania
Oscar Taylor's Butcher Bakery and Bar, San Diego, California
Sweeney's Champagne Bar, St. Paul, Minnesota
Belly Up Tavern, Sola Beach, California
South Hills Country Club, East Moline, Illinois
Hotel Coellner Hof, Cologne, Germany
Night of the Rest Hotel, Burlington, Vermont
Night Stage: The Finest in Live Blues and Jazz, Cambridge,
    Massachusetts
Miss Jessie's Soul Food, Hazel Crest, Illinois
Key Largo Restaurant and Bar, Portland, Oregon
The President Riverboat Casino, Davenport, Iowa
ETAP International Hotels, Amsterdam, The Netherlands
Lascaux, San Francisco
Memphis, Philadelphia, Pennsylvania
Plus thirty others

· *13* ·

Conclusions

This biography of Pat Patrick is a musical life story. We tried to follow as closely as possible the information revealed in the archival materials, the narrative of Pat's activities, interspersed with Pat's own quotations, clippings, performance announcements, reviews, and photographs. We supplemented as we could with discussions with family members and friends. In this biography, we lift up to the world a musician who was not famous or well-known. He was a sideman. Yet in this role, his impact was deeply felt and his voice was powerfully heard even if his face was not always seen.

We wanted to give Pat a chance to tell his own story and we hope that we did that. Pat Patrick worked within a historical framework of popular music and during a time when two generations were at odds about the social and aesthetic forces that would define an emerging era.

His musical work came at one of the most critical points in our sociocultural history, the 1960s and 1970s. This was a time when so many questions, values, and ideas about what would define American life were being explored. Pat Patrick was a thinker, and he struggled to put his ideas forward and to make his artistic mark. He sought to fill in gaps with great music practice that ensured that some of his best efforts would represent and survive. His story is an example of the experience of living that demands struggle, the pursuit of dreams, and the effort to be the best that one can be.

Pat, we thank you for all your human sharing.

• *14* •

Song for Amiri

*T*ragically, Amiri Baraka passed as we were finishing this book celebrating his dear friend, Pat Patrick.

Amiri Baraka was our griot, teacher, mentor, and friend. We love you and we thank you.

The two things he would jokingly say to me during these last two years were, "That's the gig," and "Who got next?" implying responsibility.

The best we can do to honor him is to work as artists and teachers with the inspiration he ignited within each of us and to give some maps to a younger generation to help them find their path.

Amiri found a path to our destiny in great Black, sweet, deep music.

Oh Amiri, oh Amiri, what shall we do now that you are no longer with us? The poet who taught us how to think, ask questions, search for the history in our songs, and see the news that's in the blues is gone.

We shall honor you as you honored us, with a charge, as you said, "The point is that if the music is to create with its direct beauty, the social economic aesthetic intellectual material reflection of its expressive presence, then the new work has to be done by all of us, concerned for one reason or another with that music and its future growth and existence."

Amiri,

We promise to at least work, that we can do.

We promise you that we will value truth, that's what you do.

We promise we will never forget the paths of the poetry, the duty and the power and the responsibility of the music.

"That's the gig," "we got next," that's what we shall do, that's how we hear the plays, that's how the youth will get to the truth, will know your readings, and the way you brought power and grace to the people's fuss, that's how we shall be, now that you live in us.

Amiri, we thank you!

Bill Banfield with Amiri Baraka.
From the Pat Patrick Archive

Notes

CHAPTER 3

1. John F. Szwed, *Space Is the Place* (Mojo Books/Payback Press, 1997).
2. Szwed, *Space Is the Place.*
3. Szwed, *Space Is the Place.*

CHAPTER 4

1. St. Clair Drake and Horace R. Clayton. *Black Metropolis* (Chicago: University of Chicago Press, 1945, 1961, 1972, 1993).
2. Monika Herzig, *David Baker: A Legacy in Music* (Bloomington: Indiana University Press, 2011), 3.
3. George Lewis, *A Power Stronger Than Itself* (Chicago: University of Chicago Press, 2008), 11, 12, 13, 55, 56.
4. Ellington, 1932 recording.
5. Coltrane, from Ken Burns *Jazz*, quote.
6. Parker, *Spirituals and the Blues*, 6.
7. William Banfield, *Musical Landscapes in Color* (Lanham, MD: Scarecrow Press), 156.

CHAPTER 5

1. Deval Patrick, *A Reason to Believe* (New York: Broadway Books, 2011), 9, 10, 116–143.
2. Patrick, *A Reason to Believe.*
3. Patrick, *A Reason to Believe.*
4. Patrick, *A Reason to Believe.*

CHAPTER 6

1. William Banfield, *Ethnomusicologizing* (Lanham, MD: Rowman & Littlefield, 2015), 127, 128.
2. Robin Kelley, *Thelonious Monk: The Life and Times of An American Original* (New York: Free Press, 2010), 409–10.
3. John F. Szwed, *Space Is the Place*, 282–84.
4. John F. Szwed, *Space Is the Place*, 282–84.
5. Deval Patrick, *A Reason to Believe*, 116–43.

CHAPTER 7

1. Amiri Baraka, *Digging, the Afro-American Soul of American Classical Music* (Berkeley: University of California Press, 2010), 92.
2. Deval Patrick, *A Reason to Believe*, 116–43.

CHAPTER 11

1. The Pat Patrick archival materials were sent in 2007 to Boston from the storage facility where they were left since his death in 1991. Miraculously intact, the most valuable items were put away by Pat himself. Those materials make up the pieces seen in this biography, the things that have given us all of the information that we have about Pat as a living musician.

Index

Note: All page numbers in *italics* refer to photographs or illustrations.

About the Author

Bill Banfield currently serves as professor of Africana studies/music and society, director of the Center for Africana Studies/Liberal Arts, and teaches in the dept. of composition and the graduate school, Berklee College of Music. In 2002, he served as a W. E. B. Dubois fellow at Harvard University and was appointed by Toni Morrison to serve as the visiting Atelier Professor, Princeton University, 2003. Having served twice as a Pulitzer Prize judge in American music (2010/2016), Banfield is an award-winning composer whose symphonies, operas, chamber works have been performed and recorded by major symphonies across the country.

Banfield is a national public radio show host having served as arts and culture correspondent for the Tavis Smiley shows. He has authored six books on music, arts and cultural criticism, and history and biographies, covering everything from contemporary Black composers, to Ornette Coleman, Nikki Manaj, and Kendrick Lamar. In 2010, he was hired by Quincy Jones to write a national music curriculum and book for schools about American popular music culture.